SECRET
UNDER
GROUND
BRISTOL

Secret Underground Bristol was researched by the following members of the Bristol Junior Chamber:

Co-ordinator
Simon Steel

Researchers

David Brown	Chris Merrick
Margaret Cavanna	Simon Pitchers
Simon Cross	Nick Tolchard
Giselle Davies	Bob Tomlinson
Dominic Elson	John Tuffney
Louise Grant	Sally Watson
David Mortimore	

SECRET UNDER GROUND BRISTOL

Written by	Sally Watson
Designed by	Rob Hifle
Original photography by	Chris Merrick
Foreword by	Lucinda Lambton

First published by The Bristol Junior Chamber in 1991
Text by Sally Watson and all original photographs by Chris Merrick © 1991 Bristol Junior Chamber

Maps reproduced from the 1990 Ordnance Survey 1:50,000 Second
Series Sheet 172 map with the permission of the Controller of
Her Majesty's Stationery Office. © Crown Copyright

Permission to use photographs and illustrations is gratefully
acknowledged to:
Bristol Industrial Museum
Bristol United Press Limited
Bygone Bristol
City of Bristol Engineers Main Drainage Department
City of Bristol Museum and Art Gallery
City of Bristol Records Office for material owned by the City Council
City of Bristol Reference Library
John Cornwell
Peter G. Davey
Howells of Bristol
Don Loader
David Street
Temple Local History Group

This book was designed and produced in association with Steel Designs, Bristol
and with special thanks to Franco Paro

Printed in Great Britain by Doveton Press Limited, Bristol
Bound by W.H. Ware & Sons Limited, Clevedon
Consultants: Brokenborough Publications

British Library Cataloguing in Publication Data
Watson, Sally *1954*
    Secret Underground Bristol
    1. Avon (England). Underground structures
    I. Title   II. Merrick, Chris
    914.2393

ISBN 0-907145-01-9

Bristol Junior Chamber, 16 Clifton Park, Bristol BS8 3BY

CONTENTS

FOREWORD

"Underground" is a word quite riddled through with romance, reeking of secrecy, of hidden excitements and of the exquisite thrill in their discovery. It was with such a romantic spirit that I plunged into *Secret Underground Bristol*, and it was with such thrills of discovery that I plunged on, quite unable to stop: down hidden rivers; through glistening grottoes; into a cave as high as the Avon Gorge and, most gripping of all, up a steep tunnel rising through the rocks of the Gorge itself. This was built for a little railway which trundled up and down the terrifyingly sharp gradient of 1:2.2, in what was then the widest tunnel of its kind in the world.

This is a book full of such delectable delights: the tale of the stuffed hermit, of the underground moat of Bristol Castle – covered over but still navigable by boat – and of the 100-strong symphony orchestra, under Sir Adrian Boult, testing the acoustics of an abandoned railway tunnel. Most glittering of all are the grottoes and the descriptions of eighteenth century spa life at Bristol's hot wells, where "the sublime scenery of the cliffs was enlivened by the sounds of music" and John Wesley came to be cured of "a greedy consumption". The hot springs had their enemies, most notably a Dr. Thomas Beddoes, who was convinced that cows' breath was a better cure and would haul cattle into his patients' bedrooms to prove it . . . READ ON . . . READ ON!

Lucinda Lambton

 Open to the public

 Not open to the public

 Take a picnic

 Take the camera

 Scenic views

INTRODUCTION

If you think you are standing on solid ground, think again. Beneath your feet is another Bristol – a hidden city of tunnels and waterways, caves and grottoes, cellars and sewers, with a secretive life of its own.

The Bristol Junior Chamber – which is well-known for initiating imaginative events such as the Balloon Fiesta and Heritage Walks – has gone underground to reveal this mysterious city.

An enthusiastic group of BJC Members led by Simon Steel, together with professional writer and archaeologist Sally Watson, has been exploring Bristol's eerie underworld for nearly two years.

It was a journey into the unknown. There is no comprehensive map of underground Bristol, and surface landmarks are few and far between. Memories and legends were often the only signposts – and misleading ones at that. Sometimes a "smuggler's tunnel" turned out to be nothing more than a drain. But at other times a mundane hole in the ground led to something spectacular. The subterranean travellers unearthed hundreds of extraordinary places and the fascinating human stories behind them.

Secret Underground Bristol takes you on the same voyage of discovery. It is an exhilarating experience, but like all pioneering journeys, it is just the beginning. Underground Bristol still holds many secrets, and the search continues . . .

Warmley Grotto

Goldney Grotto

A VERY PLEASANT PLACE – FOR A TOAD

Grottoes

Eighteenth century Bristolians had "souls engrossed with lucre" according to Daniel Defoe. On the surface, he was right. Then, as now, Bristol businessmen were hard-headed folk. But there was more to them than that. If Defoe had dug a little deeper, he would have unearthed closet romantics, living out their fantasies in weird underground grottoes.

A grotto is the strangest of all follies – an artificial cave. Building these hidden retreats seems to have been particularly appealing to secretive Bristolians. It is surely no accident that, out of the handful of British grottoes which have survived, Bristol boasts two extraordinary examples. In Clifton, there is one of the oldest, finest and most famous in the country; in Warmley, one of the least-known and most mysterious.

Both were built in the eighteenth century – the heyday of the folly. England was littered with endearing bits of nonsense in those days – not only grottoes but sham castles, pointless columns, "ruined" towers, even a mock Stonehenge. Perhaps this rash of frivolity was a reaction against the relentless elegance and restraint of the Age of Reason. In any event, Georgian gentlefolk were infatuated with the "picturesque", and a mournful ruin added immeasurably to a carefully contrived "natural" landscape. The most ambitious folly builders

even included ornamental humans in their schemes. Hermits were in great demand for grottoes and sanctuaries, and there seems to have been no shortage. Advertisements produced a healthy response, despite the fact that average conditions of employment included living underground unshaven, unclipped and speechless for seven years. The rewards were high for any anchorite who stuck it out until the end of that mystic term, but many fell by the wayside. One exasperated employer suffered such a high turnover that he was forced to use a stuffed hermit.

Alexander Pope, who built the first true grotto in the garden of his Twickenham home in the 1720s, never had to resort to such expedients. Measuring only 4 feet 6 inches, and being a famous poet into the bargain, he was as colourful a character as any grotto could hope to entertain. Pope aimed for the natural look in his underground retreat, the better to commune with Nature and his Muse. His grotto was rough and irregular like a real cave, and was decorated with stalactites which friends had shot down like partridge in Cheddar Caves. According to Dr Johnson, Pope "adorned it with fossile bodies, and dignified it with the title of grotto, a place of silence and retreat, from which he endeavoured to persuade his friends and himself that cares and passions could be excluded".

Alexander Pope and his grotto

Unimpressed by either the place or its diminutive owner, Johnson concluded that "a grotto is a very pleasant place – for a toad!"

Nevertheless, Pope's grotto was much celebrated at the time, and probably inspired Thomas Goldney III to build an underground extravaganza in the grounds of his Clifton mansion. Happily, this superb grotto is beautifully preserved in the gardens of Goldney House (now a University Hall of Residence). It can be viewed on occasional Open Days, but go early to avoid the crowds if you can. Goldney Grotto is something to experience alone.

The entrance to the grotto is a Gothic façade built into the side of a hill. It looks innocuous enough, but passing through it is unnerving. From the civilised world of trim lawns and afternoon tea, you are suddenly plunged into a pagan underworld. Everything is bathed in the eerie green glow of moss-laden skylights, and echoes to the crash of water. The cavern is gloomy and glistening at the same time – encrusted with thousands of shells, conches, crystals, fossils and corals like the cave of some eccentric water god. You turn instinctively left, towards the sound of water – and there he is.

Far away, it seems, at the top of a narrow cleft, lounges a marble deity. From the urn at his right hand, water cascades down over the rocks, singing through the shells, and tumbles into a deep pool at your feet. As your eyes grow accustomed to the light, you see that the grotto has other strange occupants. At the back of the main chamber, a plaster of Paris lion glares sightlessly at you as he guards the den in which his mate crouches.

The Goldney waterfall

The entrance to a pagan underworld

The lion guards his den

The water god, seen from a side tunnel

From the western end of the grotto, several tunnels branch off. One is a hundred feet long and emerges at the other side of the garden. Perhaps Goldney brought visitors down this way at night, so that the candle-lit grotto would take their breath away after a long, dark walk. Another tunnel leads up behind the cascade, past the god's cave and into the bottom of Goldney Tower. This was built to house a steam engine which pumped water to the grotto's cascade and to the fountains in the lily pond (nowadays, this is done by electricity).

Thomas Goldney III expended 27 long years of effort (from 1737 to 1764) on his grotto. The outline of the main chamber was in place by August 1739 (the date is picked out in shells on the rooflight of the west hall), but there were still innumerable shells and fossils from all over the world to be collected, statuary to be commissioned and the cascade to be engineered. It is said that Goldney employed men for seven years to collect the "Bristol Diamonds" which encrust the pillars supporting the roof of the cavern. The grotto was clearly a labour of love.

It is also unique, and seems to have sprung almost entirely from the imagination of its creator. Once Pope had set the trend, grottoes did become very fashionable, but most builders copied standard models from pattern books. Goldney does not appear to have copied anything. His grotto is one of the earliest in Britain, and it is far more complex than any started at a similar date. When Mrs Mary Delaney, a society grotto-designer of repute, saw it in 1756 she declared that it was "by much the finest thing of the kind I ever saw". We can probably take her word for it. This resourceful lady once contrived to turn her ballroom into a forest, complete with a grotto and a Gothic chapel which doubled as a sideboard – so if anyone knew their way around a folly, it was she.

Why Goldney spent so much time and money on his grotto, and what he did in it, are far from clear. He was not a poet or philosopher but a hard-working, Quaker banker and business-man. Again, Mrs Delaney may offer a clue. "The master," she says, "is reckoned a great humorist". Perhaps the eccentric bachelor just

Goldney Tower and grotto entrance. The waterfall runs beneath the ground between them

Thomas Goldney III

wanted to amaze and amuse. Unlike Pope's gloomy den, Goldney's theatrical grotto is designed not so much for quiet contemplation as for gasps of astonishment and delicious chills down the spine.

The great humorist no doubt delighted in the amazement of his friends. The grotto also helped to raise his social standing by attracting well-connected visitors. This may have been a strong motivation for Goldney, because his family was far from aristocratic and had not always been entirely respectable. His grandfather (Thomas Goldney I) was a grocer, albeit a prosperous one, and staunch Quaker. His son, Thomas Goldney II, was a more adven-

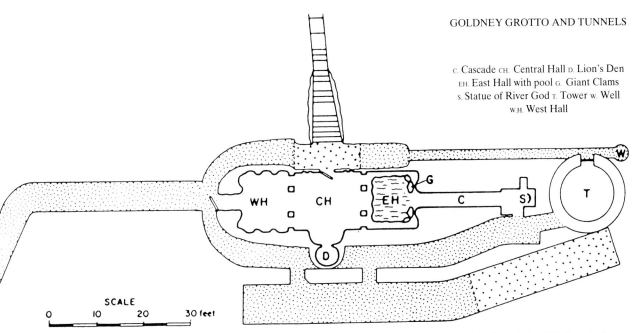

c. Cascade CH. Central Hall D. Lion's Den
EH. East Hall with pool G. Giant Clams
S. Statue of River God T. Tower W. Well
W.H. West Hall

SCALE

0   10   20   30 feet

With kind permission of Professor R. Savage

turous businessman but somewhat less devout. He built up the family fortunes and acquired the estate in Clifton, but not without sacrificing some of his Quaker principles. He had several legitimate interests, such as financing Abraham Darby's pioneering iron works, but in 1708 he sponsored a privateering voyage designed to capitalise on the war with France. The Society of Friends was deeply disturbed, but there was little they could do about it. Goldney was in prison for suspected fraud at the time.

So when Thomas Goldney III became head of the family in 1731 at the age of 35, he was secure financially, but there was a good deal of ground to make up socially. As his father

had already rebuilt the family home, he set about enlarging the estate and laying out superb gardens, complete with that most aristocratic of extravagances – a folly. If Goldney wanted to establish himself as a real gentleman, there was no better way to do it.

This still does not fully explain why the folly he chose was a grotto. The spectacular, open views from his grounds would have provided the perfect setting for a classical temple or Gothic ruin, and he could have run one up in a tenth of the time. There must be a more personal and emotional reason behind the grotto. Perhaps Goldney simply longed for adventure. In the days of his maverick father, he had had a taste of it.

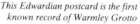
This Edwardian postcard is the first known record of Warmley Grotto

That scandalous privateering voyage, which returned when Goldney was 15, brought back one particularly spectacular find – Alexander Selkirk, the castaway who inspired Defoe's Robinson Crusoe. The Captain also collected gorgeous Pacific shells and corals which he presented to his sponsor's son – together with exciting travellers' tales, no doubt. All this must surely have made a tremendous impression on an imaginative youth like Goldney. He certainly developed a taste for the exotic if his library – which included a *Life of Mahomet* and the *Arabian Nights* – is anything to go by. Perhaps, after all, Goldney built his Aladdin's Cave primarily for himself, and whenever respectable Quakerdom became too

stifling, he escaped underground into a romantic dream world. Who knows?

Many unanswered questions linger around Goldney Grotto. But it is an open book compared with the grotto at Warmley. This strange suite of caverns is undoubtedly eighteenth century, but there is no record of when or how it was built, what visitors thought of it, or what they did there. The first written evidence of the grotto is a church magazine dated 1908, which briefly mentions it as one of the attractions at a summer fête. For two centuries, Warmley Grotto seems to have been ignored, neglected, even used as a pig-sty. It is only now that dedicated local historians are

Part of the Warmley labyrinth

The central chamber, open to the sky since the roof caved in

uncovering its secrets.

Excavation is still in progress, and the grotto is only occasionally opened to visitors, but the entrance can be seen in the public park which used to be the grounds of Warmley House. The House itself is now a private retirement home.

Fragmented though it now is, the Warmley estate is a fascinating landmark of the industrial revolution. It was established in 1746 by William Champion, who invented and patented a revolutionary new zinc-making process and pioneered integrated brass manufacture. In Warmley, he built what was probably the first self-contained industrial complex, including not only brass, copper and zinc works, but cottages for his workers and a mansion for himself.

Champion was an eccentric genius whose life story reads like a Greek tragedy. In his youth, he is said to have dressed as a pauper and travelled Europe for six years, discovering the secrets of brass and zinc manufacture. Back home, he became an industrial king, ruling over Europe's largest and most successful brass foundry. But the breadth of vision which made his fortune destroyed him in the end. His inventive mind was forever dreaming up grand schemes. In 1767, for example, he proposed creating a floating harbour in the centre of Bristol; but he was way ahead of his time, and it

*Champion's Neptune
– a giant, like his creator*

was another 40 years before this excellent idea was pursued. Eventually, Champion over-reached himself. The failure of an ambitious docks project and over-diversification stretched his finances to the limit. In 1769, his company collapsed and the Warmley works were sold to his arch-rival, Harford's and Bristol Brass and Copper Company. The new owners did very well out of Champion's inventions, and legend has it that, some years later, they sought out the ruined genius to offer him an annuity. They found him working as a mason in Liverpool but, as befits a tragic hero, he declined their offer.

Like Thomas Goldney III, Champion was a Quaker, and he was related to Goldney by marriage. He must have known the Clifton garden and grotto, and no doubt took some inspiration from them, but the landscape he created at Warmley is very different. Champion's gardens are like their creator – larger than life and workaholic. Everything is on an enormous scale, and even ornamental features are closely connected with industry. The focal point of the grounds used to be a 13-acre lake, which also served as a reservoir to feed the water mills at the foundries. It is now dry, but the immense statue of Neptune that once loomed out of the middle of it still stands. He is a crude yet powerful figure – a 20-foot giant, partly made of smooth plaster and partly of rough black clinker waste from the works.

Grotto or eccentric laboratory? Warmley is a mystery

This cascade is part of Champion's complex water system

Sheer size is the most impressive feature of the grotto, too. Built inside an artificial mound, it is a rambling network of great vaulted tunnels and chambers – some with a ceiling height of over 20 feet – which house a complex system of cascades, water channels and pools. Two of these pools seem too deep to have been made for ornamental purposes. It is likely that they were originally industrial tanks, and that practical Champion built his grotto over a redundant foundry. He also recycled the spikey waste from the zinc process to give a rough, cave-like texture to the walls. There are no shells, crystals, statues or pretty decorations. All is dark and melancholy. The only light seeps through small roof openings, except in the central chamber, which has been open to the sky since the roof caved in, probably long ago.

It is all very strange. Is the grotto simply unfinished? Maybe Champion intended to decorate it in the course of time – although one cannot imagine him fiddling about with shells and nick-nacks. The grand gesture was more his style, and the grotto may have relied on spectacular use of water, light and even pyrotechnics. Excavation has uncovered a superb hydraulic system and some tantalising evidence which may point to other "special effects". In one chamber, for example, there was a 20-foot waterfall which cascaded down from a hidden

Warmley Grotto's only decoration:
industrial waste

water-tank. On the left is a culvert leading up to the tank which appears to have no purpose. It is possible that this was used to create a pall of smoke or steam – just the sort of trick to appeal to the ingenious Champion.

But this is speculation – as is so much else about Warmley Grotto. Its many baffling features inspire numerous theories. One of the wildest is a suggestion that it is not a grotto at all, but an eccentrically designed laboratory in which Champion tried out secret industrial experiments!

Archaeology is continuing to piece together the evidence, and the story of Warmley Grotto may eventually become clearer, but until then it will remain a happy hunting ground for the imagination.

PROPER PIT COUNTRY

The Bristol Coal-mines

Deep in the ground beneath some of Bristol's most opulent buildings lies the foundation on which their prosperity was built: coal.

It is difficult to believe now, but Bristol was once a thriving mining area and rich veins of coal, honeycombed with mines, still run beneath the City. No other town in Southern England has such a resource. It gave Bristol a unique advantage and was a key factor in the City's affluence and industrial growth, particularly in the seventeenth and eighteenth centuries.

The Bristol and Somerest Coalfield is huge, running from Wickwar in the North to the Mendips in the South, from Clevedon in the West to Frome in the East. But unfor-

tunately, the coal occurs in thin seams, trapped between layers of rock, and is difficult to extract. Eventually, this made the Bristol mines so unprofitable that they were all abandoned by the middle of this century.

Thin seams were no problem for Bristol's earliest miners, because they only excavated coal which appeared near the surface or "cropped out". They were mining in this way as far back as 1223, which makes Bristol one of the first coal-producing areas in the country. It was a small-scale operation in those days, with individuals or groups extracting modest amounts of coal for use in homes and the forges of local smiths. It wasn't until the sixteenth century, when demand for coal increased, that pits were dug and the pace of mining speeded up.

By the eighteenth century, more and more coal was needed to fuel Bristol's glass, china, sugar and metal industries. Between 1670 and 1750, the number of pits doubled in and around Kingswood, which was always Bristol's principal mining area, although at some time or another pits have been worked all over the City.

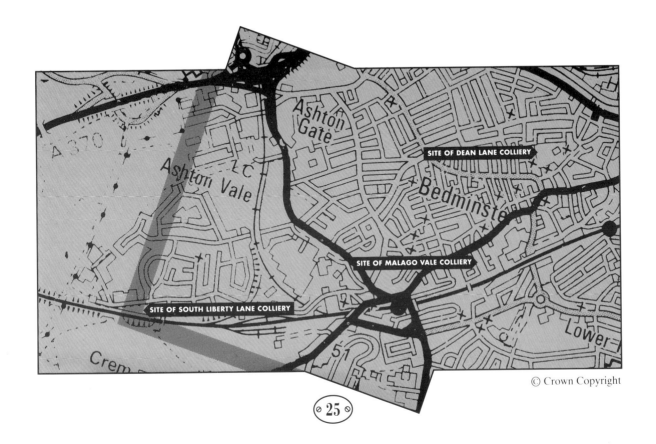

© Crown Copyright

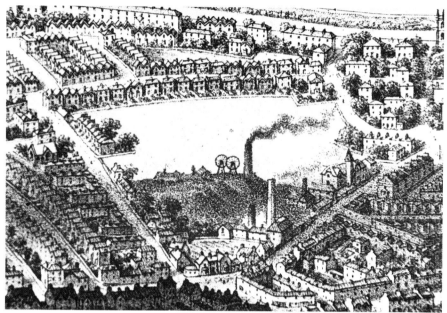

Dean Lane Pit, Bedminster, as seen from a hot air balloon in 1872

The Kingswood miners were a law unto themselves. The area had been a Royal hunting ground – and on paper still was – but hordes of "squatters" had taken over wherever there was coal to be had. They were a turbulent crowd, and the Crown more or less gave up trying to control them. They mainly worked small, shallow pits with extraordinary names like "Strip and At It" and "Flashaway". They lived a remote, primitive existence in scattered cottages and were considered little better than savages by their more civilised neighbours. Travellers gave the area a wide berth.

One man, however, made a bee-line for the lost souls of Kingswood. He was

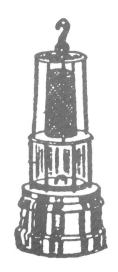

Meal break, c.1910. Miners ate little underground – heat and foul air killed their appetites

George Whitefield, a charismatic preacher and colleague of John Wesley's in the early days of the Methodist movement. On a bitter day in February 1739, he stood on Kingswood Common and, wild-eyed with emotion, delivered his message of hope to a crowd of astonished miners. Tears ran down their blackened faces. They were moved not only by his words and his obvious sincerity, but by the very fact that anyone should concern himself with outcasts such as they.

Others were not so impressed. The *Gentleman's Magazine* thundered: "The industry of the inferior people in a society is the great source of its prosperity. But if one man, like the Rev. Mr Whitefield, should have it in his power, by his preaching, to detain five or six thousands of the vulgar from their daily labour, what a loss, in a little time, may this bring to the publick! For my part, I shall expect to hear of a prodigious rise in the price of coals about the city of Bristol, if this gentleman proceeds, as he has begun, with his charitable lectures to the colliers of Kingswood."

The well-to-do expected the masses to know their place and take their spiritual comfort from gin. Uplifting religion was as dangerous as education to the status quo, and the Methodists encountered outraged opposition. They were not intimidated, and John Wesley himself worked amongst the miners, organising a school for poor

Easton Colliery, c.1890. The miner's only light is the candle strapped to his head

children and classes for adults. It was uphill work, but Kingswood became one of the first places in England where Methodism took root.

In the nineteenth century, coal-mining in Bristol reached the peak of its productivity. Modern, deep mining took over from small, shallow pits, and that meant the end of "independent" miners like the Kingswood tearaways, and the rise of big pit owners. One of the most attractive of these was a flamboyant character called Handel Cossham. He was a preacher turned colliery clerk and self-taught geologist of considerable talent. His contemporaries scoffed when he formulated scientific theories about the lie of the Bristol seams, but

South Liberty Pit, c.1900. The men now have lamps instead of candles

were forced to eat their words when he proved to be correct. Cossham's discoveries of fresh coal deposits made him an enormously rich man and Lord of the Manor of Kingswood.

In 1887, there were 17 pits in the Bristol field, employing about 2,500 underground workers and producing around half a million tons of coal a year. It was a small output compared with that of South Wales, but big enough to supply most of Bristol's needs. Shafts were sunk deeper and deeper – as low as 1,464 feet in the case of the aptly named Deep Pit in Kingswood – and workings fanned out for miles around these shafts. Tunnels were driven so far along seams that separate mines sometimes joined up.

Workings from the South Bristol pits – situated around Ashton and Bedminster – extended right under the River Avon. In fact, the workings from Bedminster's Dean Lane Colliery came within a few hundred yards of joining those from Easton Colliery, although the pitheads were a full two miles apart. The City Centre is built over a maze of exhausted workings, even though no shafts were ever dug there.

The geology of the Bristol coal seams meant particularly appalling conditions for the miners. Once they had been lowered by cage down the shaft, they often still had miles to walk to the coal-face. There they remained, in total darkness apart from their candles or lamps, for

Bristol miners spent whole shifts bent double in narrow seams

eight-hour shifts. The seams were so narrow that men often had to work on their knees, or even on their backs, in a space no more than two or three feet high. When mechanical cutting equipment was developed, it was useless in such cramped conditions. Right to the end, most Bristol coal was hand-dug with pickaxe and shovel, and hauled to the bottom of the shaft by pony.

Ventilation was very poor in most pits, and many men stripped to a pair of shorts for work because of the unbearable heat. Worse still, gasses such as "firedamp" (methane) could build up, causing dreadful explosions. One such, which occurred at the Dean Lane Pit in 1886, killed ten men. Eight more were burnt or blinded. Half of these casualties were teenagers, and three were only 15 years old.

Flooding was another ever-present danger, and the death toll in the Bristol pits was high. Until well into the twentieth century, there was little hope of compensation for widows, orphans or the disabled, as most of the local pit-owners were less than generous. Their attitude to fatal accidents is particularly revealing.

As a mark of respect, the whole pit traditionally stopped work for 24 hours when a death occurred; in Bristol, that meant every man was docked a day's pay.

Tight-fisted owners, combined with low productivity, always kept wages low in the Bristol pits. Even in 1914, the average Bristol miner earned only 5s 6d (27p) a shift – one fifth lower than the national average.

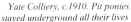

Yate Colliery, c.1910. Pit ponies stayed underground all their lives

A rare break. Like many miners, the man on the right worked almost naked

In an effort to improve pay, safety and conditions, the Bristol pits were strongly unionised towards the end of the nineteenth century. A guiding light in this movement – and one of the most loved and respected men in Bristol's recent history – was Charlie Gill.

Mr Gill was born in Bedminster in 1871. There were 14 mouths to feed in his family, so at the age of 11 he had to start earning. The only choice was to go down the pit and he worked underground for the next 31 years. In a small cottage, he raised seven children with his wife Florence, who supplemented the family income by sewing waistcoat buttonholes at one penny (0.4p) a hole.

In many ways, his was the life of a typical Bristol miner. But Charlie Gill was no ordinary man. He had a great thirst for knowledge, and in his scarce spare time he studied for a local degree in mining at Technical College. His thirst for justice was even greater, and he fought for the rights and welfare of miners and their families for 50 years. His intelligence and compassion won the respect even of his adversaries. In 1947, the former pit boy was elected Lord Mayor of Bristol and he was later awarded the MBE and CBE.

The unions gradually won improved conditions for the Bristol miners, but when it came to saving their jobs, they were fighting a rearguard action. The thin seams of coal became more and more uneconomical to mine, and the Bristol pits simply could not compete with the Northern coalfields, where new coal-cutting machinery could be used on more accessible seams.

One by one, the pits closed – Malago Vale and Easton before the turn of the century, Ashton Vale and Dean Lane by 1914, and the last works (at Speedwell) in 1936. There was a short flicker of revival when a modern drift mine was opened at Harry Stoke in the 1950s, but it was finished by 1963. In North Somerset, mining continued a little longer, and it was not until 1973, when the Writhlington pit closed, that the very last coal was extracted from the ancient Bristol and Somerset Coalfield.

The Bristol mines have been closed for only a few decades, but it is almost as if they had never been. The pitheads have been demolished

South Liberty Pit, 1923

Easton Colliery. Coal was hauled miles to the pit head

and even the sites are difficult to locate. It is hard to imagine, for instance, that the pretty bandstand in Bedminster's Dame Emily Playpark stands over the Dean Lane pit shaft, scene of so much horror in 1886. Miners' cottages, too, are now hardly recognisable. They have been upgraded into desirable period properties, with the outside privy and tin bath long since replaced by the avocado suite.

Pub names are one of the few enduring relics of Bristol's mining heritage. When you come across a Miners' Arms or Jolly Collier, you can be sure there was a pit nearby. This may well have been where the miners were paid their wages, and is almost certainly where they

*South Liberty Pit, Bedminster,
looking towards Clifton, c.1905*

spent a good deal of them at the end of a back-breaking, filthy week.

On the surface, centuries of hardship, drama and tragedy have scarcely left a trace. But underground, miles of dark, dripping tunnels will always remain as a memorial to the courage of the Bristol miners.

Redcliffe Caves

FROM KNICKER NITCH TO SMUGGLER'S BOTTOM

Caves

Caves are one of Bristol's best-kept underground secrets. From the vast vault of Pen Park Hole to the eerie caverns beneath Redcliffe, the region is pitted with them. Many have never been fully explored and most are seldom visited. Nevertheless, every Bristolian has a cave story to tell. Smugglers, slaves, hermits . . . legends swirl like mist around Bristol's caves.

None has inspired more tales than Redcliffe Caves – and no wonder. Exploring this underground labyrinth is enough to fire even the most sluggish imagination. It is rather like being lost in a petrified forest. Everywhere, there are great, stone "tree trunks" arching over chambers and passages which lead off into the

darkness. Here and there, incongruous walls and shafts seem to have taken root. Everything is deep red and the silence is complete.

No one knows how large Redcliffe Caves are. Behind a small, locked entrance in the cliffs on Redcliffe Wharf, accessible caves fan out for three acres beneath the streets of Redcliffe. Beyond these, walls and infill block the way, but there are certainly more caverns. Further-flung sections have been discovered over the years, and some say the Caves reach as far as Knowle and Brislington.

For the most part, Redcliffe Caves were not formed by nature. The marks of tools make it clear that they have been quarried out of

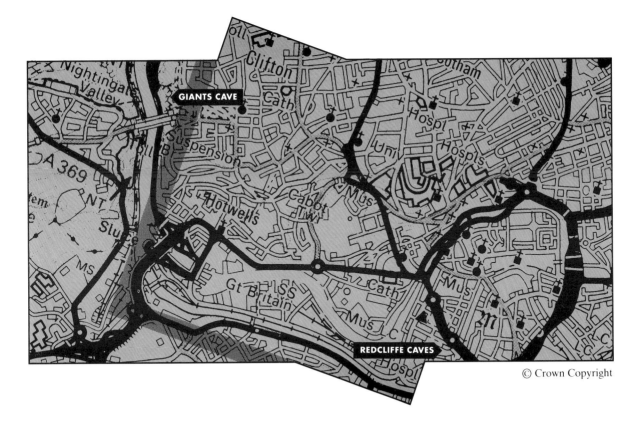

GIANTS CAVE

REDCLIFFE CAVES

© Crown Copyright

the soft red sandstone from which Redcliffe takes its name. The "tree trunks" are in fact pillars of stone left standing to hold up the roughly vaulted roof. The caves are certainly man-made – but which men made them?

The first people who spring to mind are, of course, cavemen. Thousands of years ago, streams and high Avon tides probably carved out small openings in the soft stone of the cliffs. They would have been convenient places for early man to live, offering the possibility of easy DIY extension with simple stone tools. But if these caves were Bristol's first homes, any evidence has long since disappeared.

Even legend only goes back as far as King Alfred. He is said to have hidden from marauding Danes in Redcliffe Caves, and the wharf in front of them used to be known as Alfred's Quay. The story is probably a myth, but some excavation of the Caves may have taken place in medieval times. By the twelfth century, Redcliffe had become a prosperous borough and an ecclesiastical building boom was under way, including the famous Church of St. Mary Redcliffe and the long-gone Hospital of St. John. Folklore tells that the monks of St. John's carved underground passages and cells for contemplation, and it was long believed that you could get down into Redcliffe Caves through a

This 180-year-old plaque on Redcliffe Wharf bears the old name

Redcliffe Caves were dug for sand to make Bristol glass

hollow pillar inside St. Mary's. Stories as old and tenacious as these often have some basis in fact. So perhaps medieval clerics did carve out some of Redcliffe Caves – though heaven knows for what purpose.

Only one tiny off-shoot of Redcliffe Caves – St. John's Hermitage – actually appears in medieval records. This is a small cave behind an arched doorway which can still be seen in the park opposite St. Mary Redcliffe known as the Friends' Burial Ground. Here, a hermit called John Sparkes was "placed" by Thomas Lord Berkeley in 1346 to pray for him and his family. It sounds a tedious life, but it obviously suited hermits down to the ground. A succession of them inhabited the "little Tenement in the Rocke or Cliffe" until the seventeenth century. Inside, there is a gravestone dedicated to "Christopher the Monk or Christopher Birckhead", who died in 1669.

The bulk of Redcliffe Caves, however, almost certainly owe their existence to the less romantic needs of industry. Most were probably excavated for their fine sand, which is excellent for glass manufacture. Bristol developed a flourishing bottle-making industry from the seventeenth century, because the medicinal water from the City's famous Hot Well was exported all over the world (see Chapter 5). By 1724, there were 15 glass factories in Bristol, many of them in the Redcliffe area. The sandstone cliffs were the obvious place to find the necessary sand, but as Redcliffe was already built-up, it had to be mined from below, rather than quarried from the surface.

Redcliffe Wharf in the 1880s

Redcliffe Caves being used for storage, c.1890

Abraham Lloyd, who owned Redcliffe Wharf for 50 years from 1726, no doubt excavated a good deal to supply his own glass and pot factory. French and Spanish prisoners of war probably provided him with cheap labour for this task in the 1740s. It is highly unlikely that these unfortunates were incarcerated in the Caves, but there is a persistent story that, in some part of the labyrinth now lost, a cavern was once discovered which had stone seats carved around the edges and shackles on the floor. This may have given rise to one of Bristol's most enduring myths: that hordes of slaves were kept in Redcliffe Caves to await deportation.

This is almost certainly bunkum. It is true that many of Bristol's most prominent merchants made their fortunes from the shameful trade in African slaves, but they didn't soil their hands with the product. Although some kept black personal servants, they never brought shiploads of slaves to Bristol. The slaving ships sailed a triangular route. From Bristol they made for West Africa laden with gin, arms and trinkets which were exchanged for slaves. From there, they sailed to the American and West Indian colonies where the slaves were sold. Then they returned home with a cargo of tobacco and molasses. If Redcliffe Caves are haunted, it isn't by ghostly slaves.

Smugglers are more likely candidates. It seems that, towards the end of the eighteenth century, excavation of the Caves was coming to an end, and they were being used as warehouses. Only the more accessible areas would have been used, and it appears that the true extent of the catacombs was gradually forgotten. The deeper caverns, abandoned by legitimate business, would have made ideal hiding-places for contraband.

More and more of the Caves were "lost" as time went on. Some were blocked off by walls built to separate storage spaces, and others were filled with piles of waste. The Caves were used as a rubbish dump not only by glass and pottery factories but also by William Watts' famous Shot Tower. Watts was a plumber who

This map shows the accessible caves beneath Redcliffe, but many more are blocked off

The old Shot Tower

invented a method of making molten lead into perfectly rounded shot by dropping it from a great height into water. In the 1780s, he converted his home on Redcliffe Hill into a factory by deepening the well in the basement and building a tower on top. This Shot Tower continued in successful production until 1968 when, sadly, it was demolished for road-widening.

There is a story that Watts was inspired by a dream in which his wife stood on top of St. Mary Redcliffe and dropped molten lead on him through the holes of a frying pan. Be that as it may, Watts patented his process with such success that Bristol poet John Dix was moved to pen these immortal lines:

Mr. Watts very soon a patent got
So that very soon only himself could make
    Patent Shot;
And King George and his son declar'd
    that they'd not
Shoot with anything else – and they
    ordered a lot.

Watts dumped the toxic ash from his furnaces into Redcliffe Caves. This, combined with all the other masonry and debris, made large sections of the Caves inaccessible and they were forgotten. In 1868, when a tunnel for the Harbour Railway was being excavated near Guinea Street, workmen were amazed to find part of the labyrinth. Caverns apparently

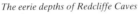

The eerie depths of Redcliffe Caves

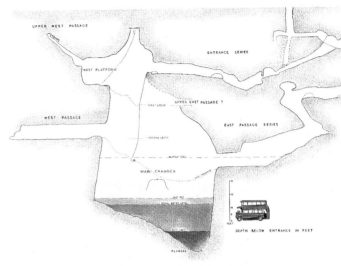

A vertical cross-section through Pen Park Hole. The bus is shown for scale

extended well beyond the far side of the trench, but the tunnel has sealed these off ever since.

Only the Caves nearest the river continued to be used. In the late nineteenth century, they provided storage space for companies trading with Africa – which may be where the slave story comes from – and in this century, for the LMS Railway. During the Blitz, some desperate citizens took refuge in the Caves, but the macabre shelter was none too safe. Bombs that destroyed Redcliffe Infants' School also opened up a crater in the caverns below.

In the 1950s, when trade in the City Docks declined rapidly, the Caves were locked up and fell into complete disuse. TV producers in search of an atmospheric setting for *Shoestring* or *Robin Hood* have been the only visitors in recent years. However, if plans to "develop" Redcliffe Wharf ever come to fruition, Redcliffe Caves may yet again be open for business – this time as a tourist attraction.

This fate will certainly never befall Pen Park Hole – an immense natural cavern which yawns beneath a field at the junction of Pen Park Road and Charlton Road in North Bristol. It is an ancient, pre-Triassic formation, consisting of several shafts and passages leading to a huge underground chamber with a lake at the bottom. The roof of this chamber is only 20 feet below ground level, but the floor drops

Professor L. S. Palmer exploring
Pen Park Hole

to an incredible 183 feet (nearly as deep as the
Avon Gorge). From time to time, the level of
the lake fluctuates by over 50 feet – though
why it should, and what its source is, have never
been convincingly explained.

Pen Park Hole was probably first
discovered by lead miners centuries ago. There is
some evidence of mining, and a few remains of
tobacco pipes and old shoes dating from around
1590 have been discovered. The Hole was already
known to be old by the time one "Captain
Sturmey, a warm, inquisitive seaman" explored it
in 1669. One of his party was "affrighted by the
sight of an evil spirit" – and who can blame him?
A huge, underground chasm with a seemingly

Cavers go down to explore Pen Park Hole for the last time in 1957

bottomless lake is the stuff of nightmares.

Nevertheless, the Hole excited considerable interest in the eighteenth century – particularly amongst clergymen. A Rev. A. Catcott, in his *Treatise on the Deluge*, cited the lake as proof that Noah's Flood had covered the whole world. He never ventured down himself, however, leaving the risky work of exploration to his brother. A fellow cleric, Rev. Thomas Newman, was not so circumspect. While peering down one of the entrance shafts in 1775, he fell to his death. It was six weeks before his body was recovered.

Soon after this unfortunate incident, the three shafts that gave access to the cave from the surface were sealed off. Since then, Pen Park Hole has entertained human visitors only once. This was in the 1950s, when plans to build up the area were put forward. One entrance was re-opened to allow various caving clubs to conduct a comprehensive survey. The entrance was sealed again and Pen Park Hole has remained inaccessible for 30 years.

The Avon Gorge is more fertile territory for cavers, and the rocks are often festooned with their ropes. The limestone cliffs are dimpled with numerous small caves on both sides of the river. Exactly how many is difficult to say. Various surveys have been published, but none is completely reliable. Cavers themselves

SEVEN-INCH SQUEEZE

Reporter John White and photographer George Edwards rest on the gorge face.

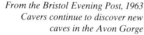

TO CAVE OF MYSTERY

Two Bristol teenagers have discovered a new cave system in the Avon Gorge.

Already it has been explored to a depth of 500ft., and is to be opened up still further.

The system is a continuation of the already known Hadles Cave. Its entrance is 150ft. above Portway.

First into the unexplored network were Ian Kelly (13), a grammar school boy and Paul Allen (18), a clerk.

They made the breakthrough at the weekend, after a year spent by cavers in clearing away mud and debris.

The initial exploration, made after a muddy squeeze of seven inches, has revealed a narrow passage high enough in places for men to walk upright and ending in a master cave.

From here, 200ft. inside the cliff, radiate two more passages.

Where they go no one knows but cavers are now planning an assault on their secrets. Many tons of earth and boulders will have to be moved first.

From the Bristol Evening Post, 1963
Cavers continue to discover new
caves in the Avon Gorge

Cavers scaling the Gorge

have added to the confusion, because they delight in bestowing original names on their "discoveries". One cave may therefore collect several names, and later be recorded as several different caves.

Fanciful names are often inspired by the extraordinary things which have found their way into caves. Take Knicker Nitch (lady's underwear) and Porno's Pot (under-the-counter magazines), for example. Since both these caves are about 200 feet above the river, and gaining access necessitates shinning up or down sheer rock, one cannot help wondering what strange compulsion drove the original owners to deposit these articles.

The Observatory, seen from the Suspension Bridge. Giant's Cave is below it and a little to the left

Some of the Avon Gorge caves have much older and more respectable tales to tell. On the Clifton side of the Avon, at Horseshoe Bend, is a large cave with a fascinating history. Its modern name is Boat Cave – because the remains of an old boat were found there – but it used to be known as the Holywell of Shirehampton or Bucklewell ("the well of bowing down"). Inside, there is crumbling masonry – the remains of an ancient shrine or hermitage – and a pool fed by a stream which seeps through the floor of the cave. The rays of the midsummer sun are said to strike the centre of this pool, and seers used to read the future in its depths. The water was renowned as a cure for

sore eyes, and hopeful visitors apparently threw offerings into the pool. The less devout no doubt retrieved these valuables later, which is probably why the rumour grew that there was hidden treasure buried in the Bucklewell.

Near the Suspension Bridge is one of the most interesting - and accessible – of all the caves. It is set into the cliff face 90 feet below the edge of the Downs, but can be approached via a 200-foot tunnel from the Observatory. This tunnel was built in 1837 by William West, the Observatory's creator, presumably so that he could enjoy the cave's breathtaking view over the Gorge. The cavern is usually known as Giant's Cave, but it has numerous other names, including

The view from Giant's Cave today

Ghyston's Cave, St. Vincent's Chapel and Fox Hole. The cave's history is equally confusing. It is supposed to be the site of an ancient chapel or hermitage, but whether this was actually inside the cave or on a ledge outside isn't clear. William Wyrecestre, an indefatigable fifteenth century surveyor of Bristol buildings, made his way down the narrow ledge which used to lead to the cave and measured the hermitage. The dimensions of the building he records are too large to have fitted into the cave, so perhaps it jutted out on to a ledge which, like the path, has now eroded away. Or possibly it was on another ledge nearby. Or maybe Wyrecestre simply got the measurements wrong (he sometimes did). Some

artefacts that were found in the cave - including, apparently, Roman pottery, church tiles and a portion of Gothic window – might hold the key to its history. But they were lost during the First World War. The only certainty is that, if any holy men lived in the cave, they were gone by 1804, when "a gang of robbers who had long been the terror of Clifton" were captured there.

The full story of Giant's Cave will probably never be established – and the same applies to most of Bristol's caves. Legends abound, but facts seem impossible to pin down.

The stories are always ambiguous, the evidence tantalisingly inconclusive. Some caves are so elusive that they actually disappear. Whatever happened to Smuggler's Bottom, for example? This reputed hiding-place for contraband is supposed to have been on the banks of the Frome at Stapleton. It's been recorded – even photographed – but nobody appears to know where it is any more.

The caves of Bristol seem determined to keep their secrets. But who would want it any other way? Mystery is part of their charm.

The view from Giant's Cave as it was in 1837. Painting by E. G. Muler

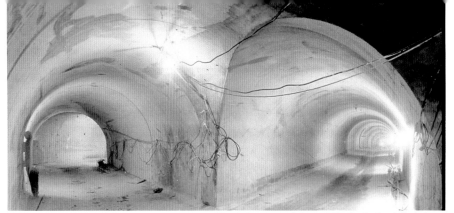

Vast drainage tunnels beneath Pembroke Road, Bedminster

FLUSHED WITH PRIDE

Sewers and Drains

Next time you step on an innocent-looking manhole cover, bear in mind that it may be all that stands between you and an enormous shaft, deeper than the Avon Gorge. When you walk down stolid suburban streets, remember that tunnels big enough to drive a bus through may run beneath your feet. And if you happen to have an allotment behind Horfield's Cranbrook Road, you may be interested to know that a vast tank of aircraft hanger proportions yawns beneath your vegetable patch.

This subterranean maze is a superb new drainage system, of which the City is justifiably proud. It is, at last, conquering an ancient problem. Bristol has grappled with inadequate drainage for centuries and, as many Bristolians know only too well, it is not so long ago that the City was renowned for devastating floods and an unsavoury pong in summer.

The River Avon was the heart of the problem. Bristol lies in a basin, drained by the Avon and the smaller rivers and streams that feed it. The Avon has the second largest tidal range in the world, and when heavy rains coincided with an exceptionally high tide, storm water simply had nowhere to go. As the Avon was also the dumping-point for most of Bristol's sewage until 1964, the flood waters which regularly invaded the City were particularly unappetising.

NORTHERN FOUL WATER INTERCEPTOR

© Crown Copyright

The new drainage system – which, it is hoped, will solve the twin problems of foul water and storm water once and for all – is now nearing completion. But it has been a long time coming.

Flooding has been a danger from time immemorial, and the sewage problem became acute back in 1809, when the Floating Harbour was constructed. Before that, the Avon and the Frome were both tidal right through the City, and the daily ebb and flow were enough to carry away most of the waste produced by a small population. In medieval times, masonry culverts were built to drain sewage and rainwater from streets into the rivers, and these served the City well for hundreds of years. Some have even been connected to the modern drainage system and are still in use today.

All in all, early Bristol was a breath of fresh air compared with many English cities. Millerd's map of 1673 is fulsome in its praise: "There are no sincks yt. come from any houses into ye. streets, but all is conveyed underground rendering the Cittie exceeding sweet and delightsom."

Unfortunately, this fragrant state of affairs could not continue indefinitely. In 1673 the population of Bristol was only 20,000, but by 1800 this figure had more than trebled. The profusion of "blood, garbage, stinking meat, dogs, cats, etc." which found its way into the

Broadmead, 1882. Central Bristol used to flood regularly

Frome and Avon was already turning the heart of the City into an open sewer. The construction of the Floating Harbour in 1809 made it into a cesspool. To compete with other ports, Bristol desperately needed a safe, tide-free harbour, so the bed of the Avon between Cumberland Basin and Totterdown Lock (and consequently the whole of the River Frome, which flowed into it) was sealed off from the tide. The Avon itself was made to run through a huge new artificial channel – the New Cut. The stagnant waters of the Floating Harbour rapidly filled up with sewage and conditions in the City became hard to stomach.

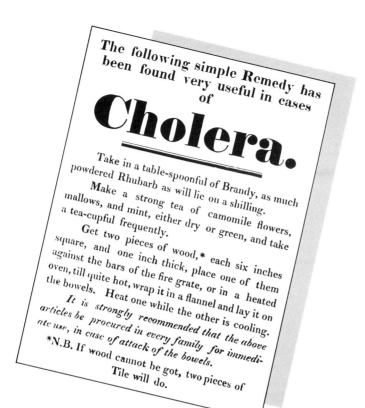

The following simple Remedy has been found very useful in cases of

Cholera.

Take in a table-spoonful of Brandy, as much powdered Rhubarb as will lie on a shilling.

Make a strong tea of camomile flowers, mallows, and mint, either dry or green, and take a tea-cupful frequently.

Get two pieces of wood,* each six inches square, and one inch thick, place one of them against the bars of the fire grate, or in a heated oven, till quite hot, wrap it in a flannel and lay it on the bowels. Heat one while the other is cooling.

It is strongly recommended that the above articles be procured in every family for immediate use, in case of attack of the bowels.

*N.B. If wood cannot be got, two pieces of Tile will do.

Desperate remedies:
health education poster, 1834

The hot summer of 1825 brought matters to a head. The "stagnant mass of putridity" in the Frome and the Floating Harbour prodded the unhappy citizens into action. They obtained an injunction against the Docks Company, compelling them to remedy the situation. The result was Mylne's Culvert (called after its designer, William Mylne). This channel was intended to restore tidal conditions to the Frome by diverting it underground from the Stone Bridge (where Electricity House now stands) into the tidal New Cut near Bathurst Basin.

Mylne's Culvert is a fine piece of engineering. It still diverts the Frome into the New Cut, and the lock gates at either end are still in excellent working order. However, it didn't really solve the problem. It partially restored tidal conditions to the Frome, but only the highest tides penetrated far enough to flush the reeking banks. The Floating Harbour continued to fester, and it is estimated that, by the middle of the nineteenth century, 34 sewers were discharging 20,000 tons of solid matter into it every year. Life was becoming intolerable – and death was becoming ever more likely. Bristol had achieved the dubious distinction of being the third most unhealthy city in the country.

Conquering floods: huge drains now
divert storm water into the Avon

Dr William Budd, physician to the Bristol Royal Infirmary, gave this graphic evidence to the Health of Towns Commission in 1845:

Along the whole course of the stream (The Frome) is a source of noisome effluvia, which in the summer season sensibly poisoned the air for a long way round . . . Between St. Johns Bridge and the Bridge at the Quay-Head, the nuisance reaches its climax. Privies up and down the stream belonging to the houses which abut upon it hang over a bank of mud the level of which is only swept at spring tide, or when the Frome is swollen by freshets. The state of things in the interval is too loathsome and disgusting to describe.

The streets were no better than the rivers, as sewer building had not kept pace with population. There weren't enough of them and many were badly constructed. Some unfortunate householders actually found themselves on the receiving end of sewers which ran backwards.

Even on the rare occasions when efficient new sewers were provided, penny-pinching Bristolians were reluctant to pay for connection. No wonder poor Sir Henry de la Beche, who conducted a survey of Bristol in 1845, found the City nauseating. He was forced to stand at the end of alleyways and vomit while an iron-stomached colleague, Dr Playfair, inspected the overflowing privies.

The 165-year-old lock mechanism of Mylne's Culvert

Conquering sewage: 200 feet below Clifton, engineers work on the last giant sewer in the new system

The Frome, c.1820
Overhanging privies drained straight into the river

Celebrating the end of 17 months tunnelling for the
Southern Foul Water Interceptor

A raging cholera epidemic was the last straw, and in 1848, the Council at last determined to clean up the City and formed a Sanitary Committee to do it. Over the next 15 years, district by district, they constructed 80 miles of sewers, which still form the bones of Bristol's drainage system. It was an impressive achievement. By 1869, *The Times* was able to report that Bristol had changed "from nearly the most unhealthy to nearly the most healthy town in Great Britain."

Although the Sanitary Committee solved the immediate problems, they were storing up more for the future. Their new system took sewage out of the streets and the Floating Harbour, but it still had to go somewhere – and unfortunately that somewhere was the tidal Avon, very near the City. Bristol's waste continued to be dumped there right up until 1964, dosed by larger and larger quantities of chlorine as the City grew, the stench rose and the river died.

The expansion of Bristol increased the risk of flooding, too. Roofs and roads throw off water – unlike open land, which absorbs it and dissipates it slowly. So in built-up areas, heavy rainfall fills streams and drains remarkably quickly – sometimes to overflowing.

By the end of the nineteenth century, it was clear that Bristol needed to solve her drainage problem once and for all, by getting storm water out of low-lying parts of the City and disposing of sewage safely.

The outlines of the modern system were first proposed in 1898, but turning the dream into reality has taken no less than a century. The first proposal was rejected by a Town Meeting, even though it had been approved by the City Council. It was put forward again in 1905 – and rejected again. Over the next 30 years, more committees, investigations and reports worried away at the problem without producing noticeable results. Then, just when it looked as though action was about to be taken, the Second World War intervened. At last, in 1959, construction of the present system began – and it is still going on. It will not be until 1998 – a full hundred years after the first proposal – that the last link in the scheme (the Northern Foul Water Interceptor) will be completed.

The Northern Storm Water Interceptor

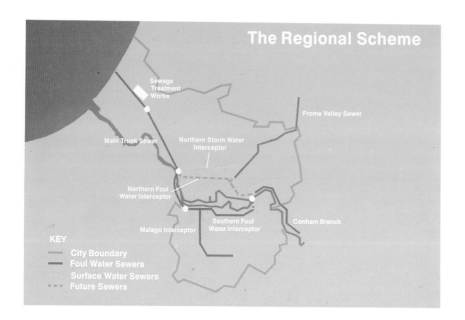

KEY
- City Boundary
- Foul Water Sewers
- Surface Water Sewers
- Future Sewers

The new system is a marvel of engineering, but in essence it is beautifully simple. The foul water system consists of a ring of huge sewers which intercept all the smaller sewers around the City and take the waste to a main trunk sewer, which runs from Black Rocks Quarry to a sewage treatment works at Avonmouth. Here, effluent is treated and discharged into the Severn.

The storm water system simply diverts flood water away from low-lying parts of Bristol into enormous drains which discharge into the Avon, well away from the City Centre.

It all sounds straightforward enough, but the structures are breathtaking in scale and sophistication. Between Leigh Woods and Black Rocks Quarry, for example, there is a gigantic inverted syphon which draws sewage from the Southern Foul Water Interceptor and takes it 100 feet beneath the bed of the Avon and up into the main Trunk Sewer on the other side.

Also near Black Rocks Quarry, the outfall of the Northern Stormwater Interceptor can be seen. This huge outfall is impressive enough, but it is nothing to what lies behind it. Out of sight, a horse-shoe-shaped tunnel seven and a half miles long, around 16 feet in diameter and up to 285 feet below ground level in parts, stretches away. Over a quarter of a million cubic yards of rock and soil were excavated to make it, and it can cope with over three-quarters of a million gallons a minute.

The Northern Storm Water Interceptor was driven through miles of solid rock

Flows even greater than this can be controlled by detention tanks such as the one under the allotments behind Cranbrook Road in Horfield. This echoing vault, with its rows of "Doric" pillars, is like the underground temple of some troglodyte sect. It is huge – 256 feet long, 59 feet wide and 2l feet high – but normally contains a mere trickle of water. If there is a sudden surge, however, a hydrobrake swings into action, the tank fills up and the flow is released slowly to prevent flooding downstream in the centre of the City. Even if 198,000 people decided to flush their lavatories at the same time, the detention tank could cope!

Bristol's watery underworld is studded with spectacular features like these. No wonder the authorities are bombarded with requests to visit the system. We all seem to harbour a secret longing to disappear down a hole in the ground. Newlyweds are particularly sensitive to the romance of sewage, and many are keen to sail off into married life on a rubber boat. Unfortunately, they can't. Most sewers are too dangerous for casual tourism. Poisonous gases, rats, disease and flooding are just a few of the risks. So perhaps it is best to stay on the surface and give thanks that these horrors have at last been banished to where they belong – the bowels of the earth.

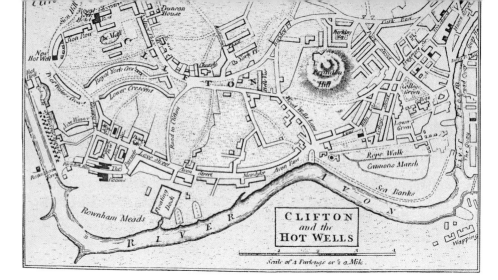

CLIFTON
and the
HOT WELLS

Scale of 4 Furlongs or ½ a Mile.

HOT LIVERS, FEEBLE BRAINS AND RED PIMPLY FACES

The Hot Springs of the Avon Gorge

One of Bristol's most fascinating subterranean features is not merely underground, but underwater a good deal of the time. The hot spring that once made Bristol a world-famous spa discharges beneath the level of the Avon for all but one and a half hours a day at low tide. For this short period, it is possible to see it gurgling out of the river's muddy banks below the Portway at the foot of St. Vincent's Rock.

Insignificant as it may look, this is no ordinary spring. The water emerges hot (76°F), effervescent and (according to an analysis conducted in 1912) 170 times more radioactive than the public water supply. Apparently, first-time drinkers of this unusual brew experienced

something akin to intoxication. This startling property was taken as a sure sign of medicinal powers, and for centuries Bristol's Hot Well was believed to cure everything from diabetes to consumption.

This faith may seem naïve, but it is understandable. Until well into the nineteenth century, people were inclined to clutch at straws when it came to their health – and with good reason. Medical science tended to be a hit or miss affair, heavily reliant on savage surgery, bloodletting and leeches. No wonder everyone longed for gentler and surer remedies.

Whether the waters of Bristol's Hot Well have any true medicinal benefits has never

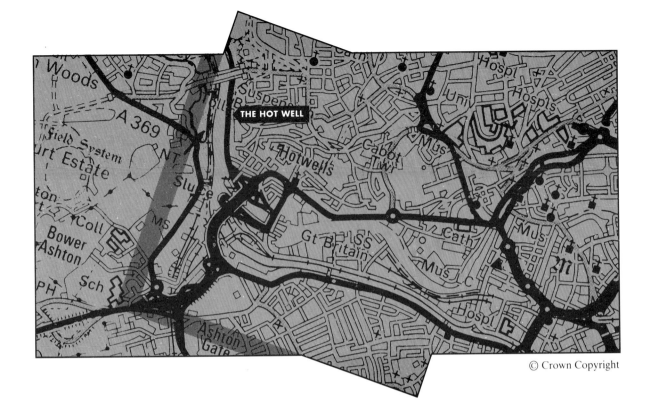

THE HOT WELL

Hotwells

Gabot

© Crown Copyright

been proved one way or the other. But to bathe and take the waters in the spectacularly beautiful setting of the Avon Gorge must have been a pleasant experience. Rest, fresh air and optimism may indeed have worked wonders.

The Hot Well's history goes back at least as far as the fifteenth century, when scurvy-ridden sailors appear to have pinned their faith on it. By 1630, the spring's reputation had grown to such an extent that one John Bruckshaw decided to cash in on it. He obtained a 40-year licence from the Crown to "take in" the Hot Well water and make baths for visitors.

The enterprise obviously took off quickly. By 1634, three Cavaliers from Norwich

Georgian High Society flocked to Bristol's Hot Well

reported "a good store of company" at the Hot Well. Visitors washed in the well and drank the water after descending the "rocky and steep-winding and craggy way neere 200 slippery steps", which led to the spring. In view of the intoxicating effects of the water, the journey back must have been fraught with hazard. Even the doughty Cavaliers admit to having "laid aside our commanding postures".

Luckily, the less athletic could also benefit from the waters in bottled form. Unlike Bath Spa water, it kept well, and by the end of the seventeenth century it was being sent all over the world. Bristol's flourishing glass-making industry was based on the huge demand for bottles which this trade created.

The increasing fame of the Hot Well attracted the attention of the Society of Merchant Venturers, and in 1676 they purchased it along with the Manor of Clifton. For some years after, the fortunes of the spring were mixed. Because its outlet is usually below the level of the Avon, keeping the spring water uncontaminated by the sewage-laden river was a continual battle, and several attempts were made to solve the problem with indifferent success.

On the other hand, the reputation of the spring as a cure grew apace. In 1677, Queen Catherine of Braganza, the unfortunate wife of Charles II, bestowed royal patronage by sampling the waters. Three years later, the spring received an even greater boost in the humble shape of Mr Gagg, a diabetic baker of Castle Street. One night he dreamt that he must drink the Hot Well water, and he wasted no time in turning the dream into reality. According to Mr

The Hot Well complex in 1791, viewed from the other side of the Avon. Painting by Nicholas Pocock

There was always fierce rivalry between Britain's spas

HARROGATE v. HOTWELLS

Mr. J. H. Howell, J.P.,—" Very sorry, my lord, that your health necessitates your leaving us for a time ; in the meanwhile can we send you on a few bottles of our own brew ? "

Gagg, he was cured within days. This case became so famous that the Hot Well grew to be regarded as an infallible cure for diabetes.

It was believed to be excellent physick against numerous other conditions, too, and the first medical book on the Hot Well, published in 1703, gives a formidable list, including "hot livers, feeble brains and red pimply faces".

In 1695, the Merchant Venturers granted a 90-year lease on the Hot Well to Charles Jones, a soap boiler, and Thomas Callow Hill, a draper, for an annual rent of £5, on condition that they spend £500 on developing the area. This was to include a pump room, lodging houses and walks giving better access to the well. How-

ever, to protect the spring from contamination, Messrs Jones and Hill had to invest in an elaborate system of pumps and valves which raised the outlet above high water mark. This left little cash to spare for stylish architecture, so the pump room was a cheap, unimpressive, barnlike structure.

Nevertheless, it became the scene of many a glittering society function, and when an elegant Assembly Room was added to the facilities in 1723, the Hot Well attracted more and more fashionable pleasure-lovers as well as invalids. High Society flocked – including the Duchess of Marlborough, the Duchess of Kent, Lady Diana Spencer and Lord Romney. They disported themselves at lavish breakfasts, evening balls, and outdoor entertainments such as ferry trips to Long Ashton for strawberries and cream, tandem rides on "double horses" and river cruises with musical accompaniment.

The resort's success meant more lodging-houses were needed, and building began in Dowry Square in the 1720s. Many fashionable medical men set up in practice here, and it became a kind of a local Harley Street.

Theatre was all the rage, and in 1729 a playhouse was built at Jacobs Wells. It was conveniently sited next to The Malt and Shovel ale house, and a hole was made in the party wall so that refreshment could be passed through to spectators and actors.

Meanwhile, a more austere type of visitor was being attracted to a rival hot spring situated on the Avon Gorge a little further from the City. This spring, known as the New Hot

The "sublime scenery" around the Hot Well. Painting by J. M. W. Turner

The only remains of St. Vincent's Spring

Well (later St. Vincent's Spring), produced a similar water, though slightly cooler and less radioactive. It was first developed around 1730, when a pump room and lodging house were built. As the only access to the spring was via a rocky horse track from Durdham Down, it only attracted visitors of stoic character and sound limb. The most famous of these was John Wesley, the founder of Methodism, who in 1754 came to drink the waters "free from noise and hurry". The proprietors made the most of his visit. They trumpeted his recovery from what they claimed was "a greedy consumption (which) had determined to put an end to his days". Wesley himself attributed his cure to a combina-

tion of the waters with a "plaster of brimstone and white egg and that old, unfashionable medicine, Prayer".

St. Vincent's Spring enjoyed a brief vogue, but it could never compete with the Hot Well. Access was dangerous for invalids, and the lonely location was hardly conducive to pleasure-seeking. One dejected visitor wrote: "The nearest dwelling is a mile distant and the only human objects ordinarily visible are the gibbeted remains of two murderers."

By the end of the eighteenth century, St. Vincent's Spring had had its day. The pump room and lodging house had been "converted into a hovel" for the workers at nearby Black

The Colonnade

Rock Quarry. Never again was the spring to attract famous visitors, but in the nineteenth century attempts were made to tap its waters for the supply of Clifton and the surrounding areas. In 1894, a public drinking fountain was also installed, and this was still operational into the 1960s. By 1975, however, the pipework had been vandalised and the tap was out of commission.

Today, the only surface evidence of St. Vincent's Spring is a spout set into a stone, which emerges from the cliff face next to the Portway near Black Rock Quarry. In a dilapidated shed above are the rusting remains of a pumping engine.

While St. Vincent's Spring faded out in the latter half of the eighteenth century, the original Hot Well enjoyed the heyday of its popularity. Trade was so brisk that a second Assembly Room was built, and in 1785 The Colonnade – a kind of shopping mall – completed the facilities. Part of this building can still be seen beside the Portway.

The Hot Well's incomparable setting in the rugged grandeur of the Avon Gorge was the secret of its success. Such scenery was irresistible to the generation which had discovered the charm of the picturesque. Being inexpensive into the bargain, the spa embodied the eighteenth century ideal of "elegant economy".

The Pump Room was "all day long the resort of invalids"

The Hot Well was a summer resort, unlike Bath, so there was no direct competition. Many tradesmen and clients moved from one to the other as the seasons turned, and the two spas complemented each other very nicely. Bath was rather formal and aristocratic, while the HotWell had a free and easy – not to say risqué – charm.

Dr Andrew Carrick wrote of the scene in 1786:

It was then during the Summer one of the best frequented and most crowded water places in the Kingdom. Scores of the nobility were to be found there every season . . . Three extensive taverns were constantly full and two spacious ballrooms were profitably kept open. There was a well attended ball, a public breakfast and a promenade every week, and often twice a week. The pump room was all day long the resort of invalids . . . The adjoining walk was filled with fashionable company; the sublime scenery of the cliffs was enlivened by the sounds of music; the downs and the avenues to The Hot Well were filled with strings of carriages and with parties on horseback and on foot.

A plaque in Dowry Square commemorates Humphry Davy

The Hot Well became so famous that it was immortalised in literature. Fanny Burney made it the setting for her vivacious novel *Evelina* and William Whitehead – a Poet Laureate of towering insignificance – published a lengthy extravaganza entitled *Hymn to the Nymph of the Bristol Spring*. For a while, the spring even boasted a real literary nymph in Anne Yearsley – a milkmaid turned poetess who operated a circulating library from the Colonnade.

In 1793, a Clifton attorney who lived on Sion Hill attempted to set up a rival spa. He blasted a 246-foot shaft down through St. Vincent's Rock and tapped a hot spring –

presumably from the same source as the Hot Well. He built a pump room (reputedly on the site of Sion House), but the enterprise quickly failed, and the water was used to supply nearby houses instead. There is now no surface trace of Sion Spring, although the bar of the St. Vincent's Rock Hotel is housed in a building erected in 1850 in an attempt to revive the spa.

The Sion Spring enterprise was extremely ill-timed, as the Hot Well itself was in deep trouble by the 1790s. Tidal contamination was again a problem, and to offset the cost of remedial work, Samuel Powell – who took over the lease in 1790 – increased charges by about 260%. As if this weren't enough, Dr Thomas

James Bolton's "Etruscan style" Pump Room was covered in advertising messages

Beddoes of Dowry Square cast doubt upon the water's ability to cure consumption. He believed cows' breath was a more effective cure, and took cattle into his patients' bedrooms to prove it. Dr Beddoes' assistant, Humphry Davy, experimented with nitrous oxide (laughing gas), so if clients fancied a change from cows' breath, they could inhale a lungful from Davy's green bag and run giggling round the Square.

Despite these eccentric activities, Dr Beddoes' views carried weight, and his contempt for the Hot Well's curative powers, together with the increased prices, sounded the death knell for the spa. Within a few seasons, the flood of visitors dwindled to a trickle. Only the desperate now came – mainly incurable consumptives nursing one last hope. A group of lodging-houses near the spring became known as Death Row, and to be prescribed treatment at the Hot Well was to be told to go away and die.

Dr Carrick, who so vividly described the bustling scene a few years earlier, gives this picture of the Hot Well in 1816: ". . . it has the silence of the grave to which it seems the inlet. Not a carriage to be seen once an hour and scarcely more frequently does a solitary invalid approach the neglected spring."

In 1822, Mr James Bolton made a plucky attempt to revive the spa. The old Hot Well Pump Room was demolished and a hand-

Taking the waters at the Royal Clifton Spa

some new building called The Royal Clifton Spa was erected. Mineral baths and spa water were provided, of course, but health wasn't the only thing on sale. Bolton hedged his bets by offering numerous other commodities, including portable seats, fossils, knife-cleaning machines, Hot Well tooth powder and boomerangs. It was a brave try, but after a short period of limited revival, the Hot Well again fell from popularity. In 1867 the Royal Clifton Spa was demolished, along with the craggy rock called Hot Well Point, to allow for widening of the river. However, the spring was preserved and the water was drawn up to a pump in a stone arch. This arch can still be seen beside the Portway.

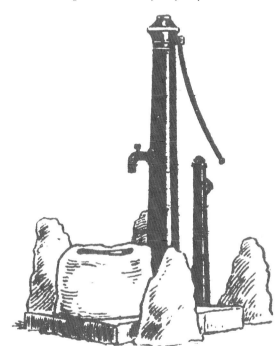

*The Avon Gorge in the 1820s, with the
Royal Clifton Spa on the right*

As the nineteenth century drew to a close, the spa seemed dead and buried. The Hotwells area, clustered around the increasingly sewage-encrusted banks of the Avon, became smelly and disreputable. Health was the last thing anyone would seek there.

Nevertheless, the enterprising Merchant Venturers, who still owned the site, were not defeated. In the 1890s, they tried once more to resurrect the spa – not in Hotwells itself this time, but on top of St. Vincent's Rock in healthy, fashionable Clifton. It would mean pumping the spring water all the way up through the Rock, but the very man to do it had presented himself: George Newnes – MP, publisher and energetic

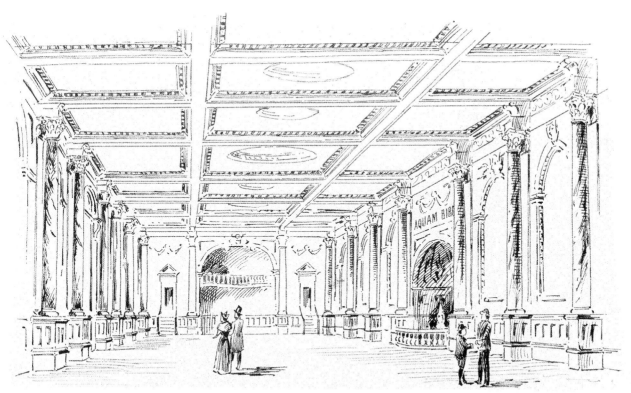

The Pump Room of George Newnes'
Hydropathic Institute in the 1890s

entrepreneur. When he applied to the Venturers to build the Clifton Rocks Railway from Hotwells to Clifton (see Chapter 6), they seized their opportunity. They consented to the Railway, but only on condition that Newnes also construct a "Hydropathic Institute" next to the upper station in Clifton.

The peeling "Corinthian Style" marbles in the Grand Pump Room as it is today

Newnes did nothing by halves, and although the Hydropathic Institute was thrust upon him, he made an excellent job of it. In 1894, he opened a spectacular Grand Pump Room, and four years later the Grand Spa Hotel (now the Avon Gorge Hotel) was built next to it. The grandiose Pump Room, with its lavish "Corinthian style" marbles and superb view of the Gorge, was advertised as "a building second to none in point of grandeur and completeness for its purpose of any health resort in the World". Nevertheless, the new spa never quite lived up to its promise. The Avon Gorge had been exotic enough for Georgian visitors, but well-travelled Edwardians found it rather tame compared with the Continental glamour of Baden Baden or Aix.

The Grand Pump Room's marble fountain dispensed its healing waters for barely 20 years. By 1920, the building had been turned into a cinema, and in the 1950s and 60s it was used as a dance hall. Now, it seems to have become an embarrassment. It is quietly rotting behind sheets of corrugated iron next to the Avon Gorge Hotel. The ruined interior is a surreal jumble. Geometric plastic chandeliers hang from ornate moulded ceilings, and huge Victorian marble maidens languish beside hideous vinyl counters from the brothel-creeper era.

Newnes' marble maidens still hold up the ceiling of the abandoned Grand Pump Room

*The fountain arch beside the Portway –
one of the few remains of the
old Hot Well*

This abandoned building, together with the Colonnade and the fountain arch beside the Portway, are all that remains from the Hot Well's long and colourful history. It seems incredibly little, but the spa's success never depended on bricks and mortar. The Avon Gorge provided a far more beautiful setting than any building. The Gorge is still there – and the spring itself still bubbles up from its mysterious underground source. So who knows? Perhaps the Hot Well is not finished yet. One day we may again take its famous waters.

Angry residents assemble outside the Clifton Spa Pump Room to voice their protest at plans to demolish the building

Spa protest fight hots up

PROTESTERS were again gathering outside an historic Bristol pump room today in an attempt to stop it being demolished.

A demonstration outside the Clifton Spa pump room at the weekend was held in an effort to block expansion of the neighbouring Avon Gorge hotel.

Objectors fear that since a High Court injunction brought by Bristol City Council was lifted last week, only a change of heart by the hotel's owners can save the Victorian buildings.

A 250-signature petition has been handed in to the hotel and a letter was due to be delivered by the Pump Room and Rocks Railway Refurbishment Group.

Newnes' Grand Pump Room has recently been under threat of demolition, but public protests seem to have saved it – for the moment.

PENNY UP, HA'PENNY DOWN

The Clifton Rocks Railway

 Travelling out along the Portway, just before passing under the Suspension Bridge, you have probably noticed what appears to be the façade of a house built into the cliff face. Look closely at this crumbling edifice, and you will be able to make out the puzzling legend "CLON ROKS RILWAY" carved into the battered lintel. This is the entrance to a forgotten engineering masterpiece: The Clifton Rocks Railway.

Funicular railways are common enough – but most are built in the open air. The Clifton Rocks Railway was – with the greatest difficulty – constructed *inside* the cliffs of the Avon Gorge. Behind the lower station on the Portway, a 500-foot tunnel rises at a sharp 1 : 2 . 2

gradient to emerge on the top of St. Vincent's Rock, beside the Avon Gorge Hotel. The upper station is that derelict, triangular building on the corner of Sion Hill and Princes Lane. It is ignominiously shrouded in rotting hardboard nowadays, but if you peer through the cracks, you can still see remnants of its former glory. The staircases, surrounded by handsome wrought-ironwork in a "Greek Key" design, still lead down to the platform. Over this, there are the remains of a pavement made of small glass panels. This was a kind of viewing platform, through which sightseers could marvel at the railway in action.

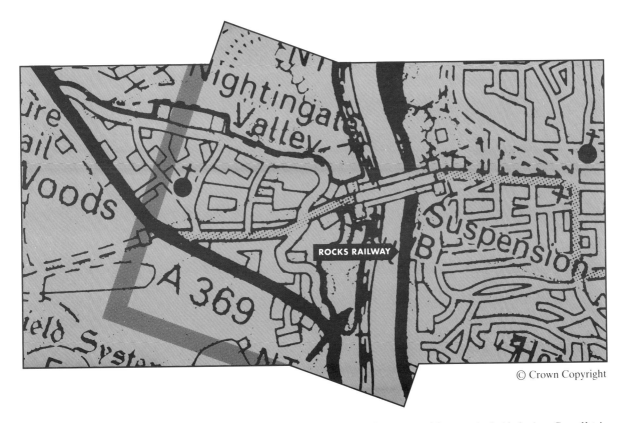

© Crown Copyright

ROCKS RAILWAY

The crumbling remains of the top station beside the Avon Gorge Hotel

The neglected state of the upper station suggests that the citizens of Clifton have scant regard for their unique railway. But then, they never really wanted it in the first place. When it was built in the late nineteenth century, Clifton was a genteel residential area. Hotwells, on the other hand, had gone very down-market since the demise of the spa. It was now a dingy, disreputable place with a shifting population of assorted seafarers. The Avon was a stinking open sewer, and the inhabitants of its banks appeared equally unsavoury to snobbish Cliftonians. The last thing they wanted was a railway to ferry hordes of drunken sailors up to their fashionable domain. In fact, they favoured complete isolation

The bottom station as it is today

from workaday Bristol, and even resisted the introduction of trams into their elegant streets.

Eventually, of course, connection with Bristol's developing public transport system became inevitable. In 1880 George White, founder of the Bristol Tramway Company, proposed building an inclined railway down the face of the Avon Gorge. This would connect Clifton with both the City Tramway at Hotwells and the terminus of the Port and Pier Railway, which ran from Hotwells to Avonmouth. The Merchant Venturers, who owned the cliffs, rejected the idea because it would be such an eyesore.

In l890, the extraordinary entrepreneur George Newnes came up with an answer which would leave the scenic beauty of the Gorge unmarred: a funicular railway running through the rock in a tunnel. The Merchant Venturers consented – on condition that Mr Newnes also try to resurrect Clifton as a spa town by constructing a Hydropathic Institute next to the upper station (see Chapter 5).

It was an irritating condition, but Newnes was not deterred. He was a man of many enthusiasms, and funicular railways were one of them. He had already collaborated with the eminent engineer G. Croydon Marks on the famous Lynton/Lynmouth Cliff Railway, and both men found conquering the Avon Gorge an irresistible challenge. Newnes put up the money, Bristol architect Philip Munroe joined the team,

The bottom station as it was, c.1900

St. Vincent's Rock. The dotted line indicates the route of the Railway tunnel

and together they planned a *tour de force* of funicular engineering.

Excavation got under way in March 1891. It was a daunting and dangerous task. At the time, the tunnel was the widest of its kind in the world, and the limestone through which it was cut was crazed with faults. In parts it was so conglomerated with other rocks that it broke the drills. In others it was so loose that tunnelling caused huge rockfalls – both inside and out. One such, which occurred just six weeks before the opening of the railway, hurtled down the cliff face and narrowly missed a passing horse-tram. This sort of thing made the workforce jittery, and it was difficult to keep men for more than a few weeks.

The tunnel was dug from both ends at the same time, and there was an awful possibility that a tiny miscalculation might mean the two shafts didn't line up properly. Jubilation broke out when, at last, they did meet in the middle, and the contractor's 10-year old son squeezed through the first hole knocked between them. But there was still a good deal to be done and, after numerous delays and crises, the construction eventually took two years instead of the scheduled 12 months, and cost Newnes £30,000 – three times the original estimate.

Nevertheless, no corners were cut and the finished railway represented state-of-the-art technology. The hard-won tunnel was reinforced with a two-foot-thick brick lining and was lit by gas lamps. Inside, four cars, connected in pairs by steel cables, were drawn up and down rails by the "water balance" technique. Each car had a tank built into the frame and, at the beginning of each journey, the top car was weighted with water so that it was heavy enough to draw up the bottom one as it descended. To get the balance right, the operator of the lower car used an electric telegraph to inform his opposite number in the upper car how many passengers he was carrying. The correct amount of water could then be added to the upper car's tank. When it reached the bottom, the water was automatically pumped back to a reservoir at the top.

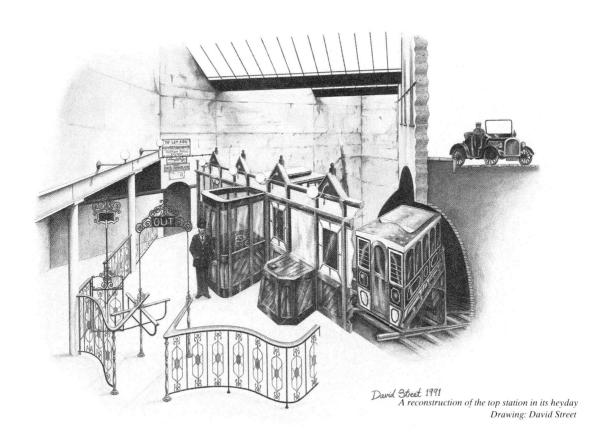

David Street 1991
A reconstruction of the top station in its heyday
Drawing: David Street

The Clifton Rocks Railway. 291.

The Railway in action

Rocks Railway ticket collectors
Photo: Peter G. Davey

Safety standards were "such as to satisfy the requirements of the most nervous of passengers". Each pair of cars had no fewer than three sets of duplicate brakes. One brake was operated by a "dead man's handle", which would stop the cars if an operator (or brakesman, as he was aptly called) let go of it for any reason. Another set ensured that the recommended speed was not exceeded. And the third was an automatic system which would operate in the extremely unlikely event of cable failure.

The Clifton Rocks Railway was a technical triumph, and caused a sensation when it opened on 11 March 1893. On the first day, 6,220 people made the return journey. Instead of a

All four carriages being removed from the defunct Railway
Photo: Peter G. Davey

ticket, they received a gilded metal medallion as a souvenir of the great occasion. Trade continued to be brisk for the first year, with around 11,000 passengers a week paying a penny to go up, and a ha'penny to go down.

Unfortunately, the railway never again reached such heights of popularity. To travel on it once was an experience not to be missed, but few people had cause to use it regularly. To go from the City Centre to Clifton via Hotwells is not, after all, the most logical route, and as buses, trams and cars made inroads even into isolationist Clifton, the Rocks Railway became a curiosity rather than a practical means of getting about.

Passenger numbers declined steadily, and in 1908 the Clifton Rocks Railway Company went into receivership. In 1912, the railway was bought by the Bristol Tramway and Carriage Company, who continued to operate it against increasingly unfavourable odds. The worst blow came in 1922, when the Portway was widened. This entailed the demolition of the Port and Pier Railway between Hotwells and Sneyd Park, which had been a useful connection for the Rocks Railway. It also brought a major road within inches of the lower station, making access difficult. In 1934, after continued deficits, the four cars were lowered to the bottom for the last time and the Clifton Rocks Railway closed.

Are they down-hearted? No! Tunnel shelterers party while the Blitz rages

But this was by no means the end of the story. During the Second World War, when bomb-proof premises of any sort were like gold-dust in Bristol, the tunnel was again called into active service. British Overseas Airways took over part of the upper section, as did a number of blitzed citizens. It was a damp, smelly shelter, in which people had to perch precariously on concrete ledges. Nevertheless, the old tunnel, with its memories of happier days, had a cheering effect. The sounds of concerts, sing-songs and fancy-dress parties drowned out the Luftwaffe.

Meanwhile, the BBC had its eye on the bottom section of the tunnel. Faced with the possibility that Broadcasting House might be destroyed by bombs or even taken over by invading Nazis, it had decided to set up an emergency headquarters in Bristol, and was on the look out for a secure base.

The BBC's first choice had been the disused tunnel of the old Port and Pier Railway which runs under Bridge Valley Road. It was an ideal site and the BBC would have been well advised to snap it up, but the Director-General saw no need for unseemly haste. Incredibly, he decided to send down a 100-strong symphony orchestra under the baton of Sir Adrian Boult to test the tunnel's acoustics before moving in. The maestro reported favourably, but the delay had proved fatal to the BBC's plans.

Bombing had now started in earnest and, because Bristol was terribly short of safe shelters, local people had taken refuge in the Port and Pier tunnel. It was wet, dark, insanitary and, as one investigator remarked, "deserved full marks for having everything that a shelter should not possess". Nevertheless, people had faith in its ability to protect them – unlike the official surface shelters. They had good reason to distrust these, as some had fallen down even before bombing started. So night after night, up to 3,000 people fought for a place in the tunnel. Despite opposition from Bristol Corporation, the shelterers became fond of their nightly home,

The emergency power supply installed by the BBC in the Rocks Railway tunnel

*The bottom station in 1941
transformed into a BBC fortress,
complete with anti-gas ventilation system*

*Rusting BBC machinery can
still be found in the tunnel*

and there was no winkling them out. On New Year's Day 1941, the BBC lined up wagons of equipment on the Portway ready to move in, but they were thwarted by a sit-in of 800 occupants. It was a clear victory for the people, and the BBC retreated gracefully.

The old Rocks Railway tunnel, despite the obvious drawback of being nearly vertical, was now the only option for the BBC. In February 1941, the four carriages were removed and construction began in the lower station and the bottom part of the tunnel. Four large chambers were built, one above the other, housing a transmitter room, recording room, control room and a studio which could take

A wartime poster still clings to the tunnel wall

around a dozen actors and was equipped for music, drama and feature programmes. Emergency supplies included hundreds of hours of canned programmes and enough food and water to withstand a siege of several weeks. The old windows of the station were blocked up, and a special ventilation plant, designed to withstand gas attacks, was installed.

The control room was manned night and day throughout the War, transferring countless thousands of programmes to various transmitters. Thankfully, the main studios at BBC Bristol were never silenced, and the emergency studio never had to be used. But just in case, whenever the bombs began to fall on Bristol, key programme staff piled into an armoured Dodge shooting-brake and made a dash for the tunnel.

The stairs leading down to the top platform

After the War, the transmitter continued to be used as a local booster station until 1960, when it became redundant and the BBC withdrew. A few years earlier, some nasty cracks had been noticed in the lower station's façade and in the tunnel behind, and the steel and concrete buttresses which now disfigure the station had been constructed to shore it up.

The Clifton Rocks Railway has now mouldered quietly for 30 years. The old stations are in a sorry state and the tunnel is filled with a jumble of relics from former uses. Concrete staircases run up each side, and between them a series of strange rooms — some of which resemble steep, narrow cinemas — remain from the tunnel's service as a BOAC store, a shelter and a BBC station. It is estimated that 27,000 cubic feet of excess brick and concrete are now resident inside the tunnel.

Nevertheless, the old Rocks Railway continues to fascinate and new ideas for putting it to good use are frequently put forward. Unfortunately, the cost of converting it always far outweighs the possible returns. It seems that the Clifton Rocks Railway is destined to remain what it has always been – an eccentric, exciting white elephant.

Part of the tunnel as it appears today

RIVER OF DARKNESS

The River Frome

For years, children have posted their Christmas letters to Santa into something that looks like a green pillar box in front of Electricity House on the Centre. Unfortunately, the only people likely to find these notes are Council sanitary officials, who can sometimes be seen disappearing, Candid Camera-like, into this mysterious structure. Inside, they climb down a metal ladder into a cramped, malodorous cavern, spanned by an ancient bridge, and sail off to inspect the River Frome, which runs unseen for well over a mile beneath the streets of Bristol.

Bristol's second river wasn't always invisible. It once flowed fair and brisk (for that is what its name means) through the City and into the River Avon. But over the years, Bristolians have forced the Frome to adapt to their changing needs. They've altered its course, blocked it up here and channelled it off there, used it as a defence, a harbour and a sewer, and finally, when it became a nuisance, they buried it. The history of the Frome is a miniature history of Bristol.

The river rises near Tetbury in Gloucestershire and flows into Bristol from the north through Frenchay, Stapleton and Eastville to St. Paul's, where it disappears. From here it flows underground past Old Market, around the north of Castle Park, under Fairfax Street and Rupert Street to Electricity House. It then runs under the Centre and out into the Floating

Harbour by The Watershed, but the original course of this last stretch of the Frome was different. It followed the line of St. Stephen's Street and Baldwin Street, joining the Avon near Bristol Bridge. Just before they converged at this point, the Frome and the Avon flowed close together, leaving in between a narrow strip of land which was easy to defend and well placed to control a natural crossing-point of the Avon. It was here that the Saxon settlement of Bricgstow ("place by the bridge") grew up, and this area remained the walled heart of the City for centuries.

William the Conqueror quickly recognised the strategic importance of Bristol, and sent Geoffrey of Mowbray to take charge of the town. He built a simple fortification which his successor, Robert of Gloucester, transformed into a huge castle that grew to be twice the size of Caernarvon Castle and one of the grandest in the kingdom. It was built to the east of the town, where the space between the Frome and Avon was narrowest, thus closing off the only access by land. The castle consisted of a massive stone keep and numerous other buildings including stables, a chapel and a fine banqueting hall, all enclosed by great walls – and, of course, a moat. To form this, water from the Frome was fed through weirs round the castle walls and out into the Avon via a great Water Gate. This meant

Bristol Castle's Water Gate

Bristol was completely encircled by the two rivers and, as one medieval writer put it, seemed to be "swimming in the water".

Bristol Castle had a rather strange history. The grim royal stronghold at first dominated the medieval town, but when the powerful merchant classes began to throw off feudal control, the castle's influence waned. By the sixteenth century it had fallen into disrepair and disrepute. The castle precinct was still Crown property and the Bristol justices had no power over it, so it became a refuge for outlaws. Within the crumbling walls, all manner of "robbers, malefactors and other inordinate livers" squatted in cramped hovels. This sordid den was a thorn in the side of the City fathers, and they longed to get their hands on the valuable site and redevelop it. At last, in 1630, the City succeeded in buying the castle, but before they had a chance to do much with it, the Civil War broke out and the castle was re-fortified for active service. Bristol came out on the Parliamentary side, but the Royalists seized and held the City for a while. This was a bitter blow to Cromwell, and may be what prompted him to draw Bristol's teeth in 1654 by ordering that the castle be dismantled. The City Council was delighted, and set about the task with a will. Every citizen was ordered to donate one day's labour a week, and within a few months the great

*Bristol Castle, c.1310, reconstructed
from archaeological evidence
by City of Bristol Museum*

fortress was no more. The area was rebuilt as Bristol's main shopping centre, and thus it remained until the Luftwaffe's incendiary bombs destroyed it in November 1940.

The bomb site has now been turned into Castle Park. Above ground, there is very little evidence of the castle – only some remnants of the banqueting hall (now rather oddly incorporated into a restaurant near the Holiday Inn) and a few fragments of masonry from the keep and the round tower. Below ground, however, part of the castle remains almost intact – the moat. It has been covered over since 1847, but it is still there, is still part of the Frome water system and is still navigable by boat.

The moat is impressively wide and deep – as you can see from the last section of it, which emerges from a brick arch near the Ambulance Station and flows into the Floating Harbour. From here, it runs underground all the way round the south, east and north sides of Castle Park. In the north were the weirs that fed water into the moat from the Frome (which is how Broad Weir got its name). Here too stood the castle mill, and the marks made by the great mill wheel can still be seen in the walls of the ancient mill tail which drove it.

The millpond area of the moat was the site of the town ducking-stool from about 1552. This barbaric punishment for nagging women

Bristol's Ducking Stool

came to an abrupt halt in 1718 when a Mrs Blake got her own back on Edmund Mountjoy, the Mayor who had decreed her punishment. "If I'm a duck, then I'll make him pay for my dripping," she was heard to shout as she went under – and she was as good as her word. Mountjoy was sued for battery, and the damages awarded were so crippling that no official dared employ the stool's services again. An enterprising businessman made snuff-boxes out of the wood and marketed them on the promise that any man who used one would be relieved of his nagging wife for ever. They sold like hot cakes.

The section of moat to the west of the castle (facing the old town) is now a dry ditch – as it probably was for most of the castle's history. It can still be traced underground, and one entrance to it can be seen in Castle Park. Near the bombed shell of St. Peter's Church, there is a sunken metal grill, beyond which 27 steps lead steeply down into the moat. This was a sally port, through which defenders of the castle could "sally forth" and surprise any attackers who might be trying to undermine the walls.

Using the Frome to supply the castle moat (in the eleventh or twelfth century) was probably the first large-scale manipulation of the river, but soon afterwards the demands of commerce prompted an even more ambitious project. By the thirteenth century, Bristol had become a busy port and the harbour facilities were no longer adequate. So in the 1240s, at the gigantic cost of £5,000, the last stretch of the

Part of Millerd's Map (1673) showing
St. Augustine's Trench

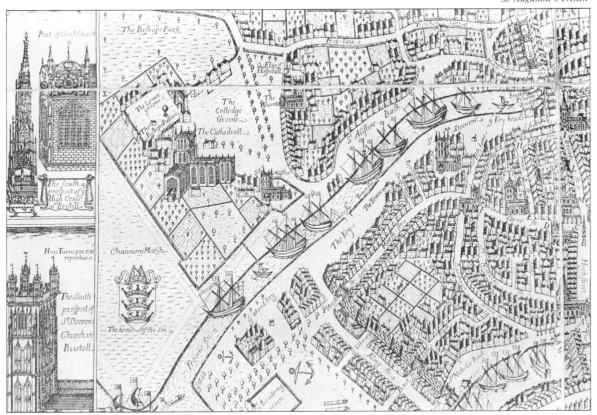

St. Augustine's Parade, c.1825
Painting by Samuel Jackson

Frome was diverted from its original course. From Stone Bridge (near Electricity House) the River was channelled into a huge new trench which joined the Avon further downstream (by the Watershed). This provided a much bigger and better harbour, with plenty of new quays and loading bays. St. Augustine's Trench, or "Deep Ditch" as it was always known, became the heart of Bristol docks and one of the most famous sights in the City. As Alexander Pope wrote in 1739, "in the middle of the`street as far as you can see, are hundreds of ships, their masts thick as they can stand by one another, which is the oddest and most surprising thing imaginable."

It sounds a prosperous and bustling scene, but there was one gigantic fly in the ointment. The Avon had a huge tidal range, as did the lower reaches of the Frome which flowed into it. At low water ships in Bristol harbour sank precariously down into the mud, and Pope's forest of masts must have lurched crazily in all directions. Bristol's "soft and whosy harborow" (as one medieval commentator described it) became more and more hazardous and inconvenient as ships got bigger and trade got brisker. By 1755, Bristol was the second largest port in the country – but was unlikely to retain this position. Disgruntled ship owners were tired of watching their craft expensively towed eight miles up the twisting, rocky Avon, only to break their backs on mud-banks in the harbour. More welcoming ports such as Liverpool were starting to filch Bristol's trade, so in 1809, after decades of torpor and procrastination, the Floating Harbour was at last constructed. The beds of the Avon and the Frome between Cumberland Basin and Totterdown Lock were sealed off from the tide so that the water level remained constant and ships could float at all times. The Avon itself was diverted through the New Cut – an artificial channel dug to the south of the City.

St. Augustine's Trench, c.1890 – still busy with shipping
A horse tram is crossing the Draw Bridge

An attempt to clean up the Floating Harbour
painted by T.L.S. Rowbotham, 1825

This solved one problem but caused another. The Frome had long been used as a dumping-point for sewage and rubbish, but the worst of it used to be swept away by vigorous tides into the Avon and, eventually, the sea. Now that the Frome was cut off from the tide, waste just collected on the river's banks, or drained into the stagnant Floating Harbour and festered. The stench was intolerable and the death rate soared. In 1825, therefore, the Frome was once again diverted. At Stone Bridge (Electricity House again) lock gates were constructed and the main flow of the Frome was channelled underground through a new culvert out to the tidal Avon at the New Cut.

The lock gates and Mylne's Culvert still regulate the Frome, and can be found, together with the Stone Bridge itself, under the green "pillar box". It was only in fairly recent times that they disappeared from view. The Frome was open all along its length until 1858. By then, a winding river crossed by 13 bridges, some of them medieval, was starting to get in the way of the traffic. So bit by bit over the second half of the nineteenth century, the Frome was covered over with great brick culverts from Wade Street in St. Paul's to Stone Bridge. Several modern thoroughfares, such as Rupert Street and Fairfax Street, are built directly over the Frome culvert.

St. Augustine's Trench (under the Centre) was the last stretch to disappear. Part of it, from Stone Bridge to the Draw Bridge (near the end of Baldwin Street), was covered over to make a site for the 1893 Exhibition and subsequently the Tramway Centre. The rest of

Disappearing into the green pillar box!

Beneath the pillar box: the Frome, lock gates and old Stone Bridge

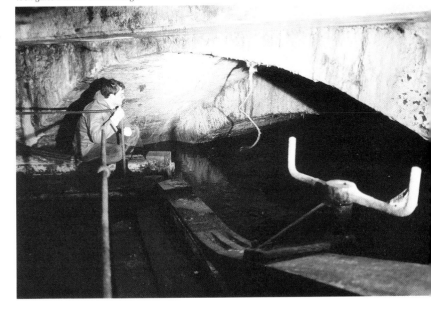

Covering over the Centre in 1938

the historic Trench was still open until 1938, and it remained a busy harbour, although the new docks at Avonmouth and Portishead were taking more and more shipping away from the centre of Bristol. It is strange to think that ships were moored in front of the Hippodrome when it opened in 1912. Appropriately, the first production was an "amazing water spectacle" entitled *Sands o' Dee* "in which enormous waves break across the seashore and horses dive into 100,000 gallons of water to the rescue of the heroine". The vast underfloor tank in which such extravaganzas were staged has been filled in, but the dolphins, anchors and ships' figureheads which still decorate the theatre are a reminder that it was once a dockside music hall. This area of the Trench was covered over in 1938, and now only the last stretch in front of the Watershed remains open.

The Frome and all the channels into which it has been forced over the years now form an eerie network of underground waterways under Bristol. It is possible to travel by inflatable boat for miles along the river, under several ancient bridges which have been incorporated into the culverts, and all the way round the castle moat. It is possible – but certainly not pleasant. The culverts are claustrophobic, smelly and attract debris like a magnet. Everything from allotment sheds to 40-foot trees get

In the 1970s, road works revealed the Frome under Rupert Street

A ship moored in front of the Hippodrome (which is still topped by a revolving dome), c.1925

washed down them. At one time, so many dead animals found their way into the system that a craft called "Dead Dog Boat" regularly went round to fish them out. It all seems a sad end for an historic river.

But the Frome is hidden, not lost, and may yet make a come-back. Many Bristolians argue that a gigantic roundabout is an unworthy Centre for their great city, and that St. Augustine's Trench should be opened up again. One day the Frome, alive with ships, may again be the heart of Bristol.

MIDDLE AGE SPREAD

Medieval Cellars and Conduits

Bristol was a medieval boom town. By the thirteenth century, it was one of the largest and richest cities in England. The port was doing a roaring trade, mainly importing wine and exporting wool and cloth, and the city was famous for huge fairs which attracted traders and entertainers from miles around. Thirteen flourishing monasteries and friaries encircled the city.

Above ground, churches are almost the sole survivors of this Golden Age. The flesh has gone from medieval Bristol – but underground, much of the skeleton remains. The city's support system was built below street level, and a good deal of it is still down there, working for a living.

Great stone cellars, built to house hogsheads of wine in the thirteenth century, are still guarding precious vintages. Medieval culverts still form part of Bristol's drainage system, having outlived many later efforts. An ancient conduit still pipes spring water into the City Centre as it has for 600 years, even during the worst days of 1940, when all the neighbouring water supplies had succumbed to enemy bombs.

This medieval underworld spreads out for miles under the streets of Bristol, but it takes some finding. A good place to start is the concrete "obelisk" in front of the Norwich Union building on High Street. This is the

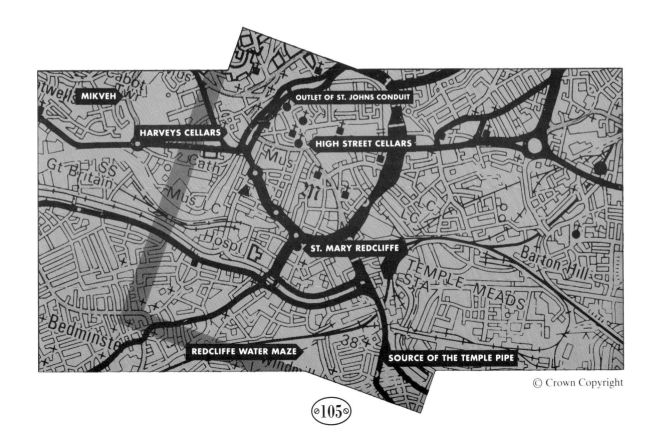

© Crown Copyright

Superb medieval cellars lie beneath the "obelisk" in High Street

incongruous entrance to some of the finest medieval cellars in Britain. Inside, a spiral staircase leads down into massive stone chambers with beautifully crafted rib-vaulted ceilings. They resemble the crypt of a Gothic church, but are in fact commercial storerooms. In the Middle Ages, merchants and tradesmen "lived over the shop". Their houses had living quarters on the upper floors, business premises at street level and storage space beneath. More care and money was lavished on the cellar than any other part of the building, because its contents would usually be far more valuable than anything above ground. Most cellars were massively constructed from expensive stone, unlike the flimsy wooden

houses which topped them. Fire swept through medieval towns so regularly that houses were almost considered disposable items, but their cellars were designed to outlive them. Those under High Street probably served a succession of buildings over the centuries.

The whole of central Bristol used to be honeycombed with similar cellars. William Wyrecestre, a fifteenth century surveyor who spent years painstakingly measuring and describing every building in Bristol, records unbroken chains of them beneath the houses of street after street. Many extended right out under the road, and for many years wheeled traffic was banned from the busiest thoroughfares in case they collapsed under the weight. It was probably an unnecessary precaution – these cellars were built to last, and many even survived direct hits in the Blitz. Several still exist under Castle Park, including the cellars which belonged to Simon Oliver, who was Town Clerk around 1400.

Unfortunately, developers have often succeeded where the Luftwaffe failed, and many of the City Centre cellars have been destroyed – including the fascinating two-storey ones uncovered quite recently beneath the old Central Post Office in Small Street. Nevertheless, many survive, particularly under Small Street and Corn Street. Some are still in active service as restaurants, clubs and storerooms. If you dine at Fosters Rooms, or down a few glasses at Pope's Wine Bar, you are in the heart of medieval Bristol.

Some cellars still house wine, as they probably did when they were built. Bristol has been the centre of the wine-importing business since the twelfth century, and two of the City's oldest wine traders – Avery's and Harveys – appropriately make use of medieval cellars.

Until recently, Avery's extraordinary, multi-level catacombs were shrouded in mystery. One upper chamber was used for wine storage,

Harveys' cellars, where their famous
sherries were bottled until the 1960s

A pre-War photograph of one of the cellars now buried beneath Castle Park

but the rest had long lain empty. Even staff were unwilling to explore these uncharted depths, so the Temple Local History Group was asked to investigate. The Group surveyed a huge maze of cellars, running not only under Avery's but out under St. George's Road as far as the Masonic Hall and under Frog Lane a far as the Council House. Blocked entrances on both sides of Park Street make it clear that passages used to extend beneath here as well. Used by wine merchants for centuries, the cellars contain fascinating evidence of forgotten practices. A great stone trough for washing casks and a ramp carved with shallow niches (to keep rolling barrels in check) are probably very old, while a section of broad gauge rail is obviously a later addition. Some highlights in the cellars' history are documented – in 1726, for example, buyers came here to view casks captured from French ships – but the full story is unclear. Exactly how old the cellars are and how far they extend beyond the many blocked passages is still a matter of guesswork.

Harveys' cellars, on the other hand, are the best-known and most accessible in Bristol. Under the company's head office in Denmark Street, a labyrinth of vaults and tunnels fans out under Union Street and Orchard Street and up as far as the Hatchet Inn. Harveys acquired these ancient cellars along with their Denmark Street premises when the company

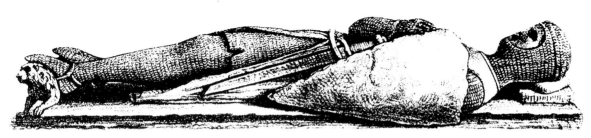

Robert de Gourney's effigy, which lies in the Lord Mayor's Chapel

was founded in 1796, and they remained the heart of the business until 1960. This is where the great casks were stored and the famous Bristol Milk and Bristol Cream sherries were bottled. Since Harveys moved their production facilities to the outskirts of the City in 1960, only a small section of the cellars has been used for storing fine wines. The rest of the network now houses Harveys Restaurant and their unique Wine Museum – both well worth a visit.

Harveys' vaults were originally the storerooms for the Hospital of St. Mark (usually known as the Hospital of the Gaunts), founded by Maurice Berkeley de Gaunt in 1220. The Berkeleys were a prominent local family and great endowers of religious and charitable institutions. In 1142, Maurice's grandfather, Robert, had founded the nearby Abbey of St. Augustine (the church of which is now Bristol Cathedral). At first, the Hospital of the Gaunts was an off-shoot of the Abbey, with just one chaplain and a modest remit to supply 45 pounds of bread a day to 100 poor citizens. However, Maurice's heir, Robert de Gourney, transformed The Gaunts into a full religious community, independent of the Abbey. Relations between Hospital and Abbey were from then on always strained, and the two were forever wrangling over rights to the land between them, which is now College Green. At the Dissolution of the

Howells store wine in the two-storey cellars where John Foster, Mayor of Bristol, stored his in the 1480s

Monasteries, Gaunts Hospital disappeared, apart from the chapel (which was sold to the City, and is now the Lord Mayor's Chapel) and the Master's House, which became a school and later Harveys' premises. Part of this building survived until the Blitz razed it to the ground, leaving only the cellars intact.

The monks of Gaunts Hospital needed extensive cellars for their stores of wine, ale and food. The community was small, but it had many dependants to support. The brothers kept up the tradition of feeding 100 needy citizens as well as maintaining 12 poor boys as resident scholars. They also provided a kind of "retirement home" for humble folk, who donated such land as they

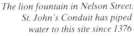
The lion fountain in Nelson Street.
St. John's Conduit has piped
water to this site since 1376

possessed in return for their keep. In fact, Gaunts was a "hostel" rather than a "hospital" in the modern sense, but poverty and sickness often go together, and the good monks no doubt tended the afflicted as best they could. Medical knowledge was pretty limited in the Middle Ages, but they probably administered simple remedies along the lines of this medieval prescription for tooth-ache:

> Take a candle of mutton fat mingled with the seed of sea holly; burn the candle as close to the tooth as possible, holding a basin of cold water underneath. Worms gnawing the tooth will fall into the water to escape the heat of the candle.

Medicine may not have been the monks' strong point, but hydraulic engineering most certainly was. All the religious establishments in Bristol built complex conduit systems to pipe in clean, fresh water from the springs in the surrounding hills, together with drains to take waste into the rivers. Much of this underground network still exists, and some parts are still in working order.

The monks needed fresh water not only for drinking, but also for washing. The Middle Ages were not as dirty as is sometimes supposed, and in sanitation – as in everything else – the monasteries led the way. Unlike St. Agnes (who was proud to die unwashed at the

The tunnels and tanks of St. John's
Conduit beneath Park Street
Drawing: David Jago

age of l3), most religious orders placed cleanliness next to godliness. They had strict cleansing routines: hand-washing before and after meals, foot-washing on Saturdays, head-shaving every three weeks and full baths several times a year. Well-behaved brethren had warm baths, but any who, like Aldred of Fountains Abbey, were troubled by "worldly thoughts", might be prescribed a cold dip. The rigid monastic timetable even laid down set times for going to the lavatory, and every community would have a "necessary house" with long rows of seats to accommodate the throng, and a stream or drain running underneath it. The drain recently excavated under St. Augustine's Abbey (the

Cathedral) seems to have served the kitchens and lavatories, and to have been placed below the conduit outlet, so that it could be vigorously flushed from time to time.

Many of the sophisticated conduit systems which Bristol's monks and friars built to service their cleanly habits still run beside the gas pipes and electric cables under modern Bristol. The best-known of these systems is St. John's Conduit, which still brings water down from an underground spring at the top of Park Street to the Church of St. John on the Wall in Nelson Street, where it pours out of the mouth of a stone lion's head set into an arch in the wall. This conduit was built in l267 to supply the Carmelite

The head of Redcliffe Pipe in Knowle

Friary which stood on the site of the Colston Hall, and a branch pipe was added in 1376 to supply St. John's. Thanks to a recent survey by the Temple Local History Group, we have a clear idea what this conduit looks like, and can trace the course of it all the way down Park Street via marker stones set into the pavement.

St. John's Conduit starts at a large well which lies under the pavement outside the triple-arched façade of George's main book shop. From here, the water itself flows down the hill through a fairly small pipe, but this passes through impressive masonry tunnels, large enough for men to walk through and repair the system whenever necessary. The pipe was

originally lead, although much of it has been replaced by later iron piping. There are a number of great cisterns and tanks along the length of the conduit, and several "dipping holes" from which local people have scooped water during various periods. At the time of the great 1865 drought, so many Park Street householders tapped into the system that the outlet at St. John's almost ran dry. This prompted the authorities to survey and restore St. John's Conduit, and to replace the remains of the old outlet with the lion's head fountain. The ancient water supply has continued to serve the people of Bristol faithfully, and during the Blitz it came to the rescue more than once. Fire-fighters used the cisterns to

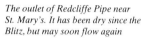

The medieval tub

douse blazing Park Street, and for a while St. John's fountain was the only source of fresh drinking water in the City Centre.

Sadly, bombing did not leave all the medieval conduits unscathed. Redcliffe Pipe, which was laid from a spring in Knowle to St. Mary Redcliffe in 1190, flowed unchecked until 1941, and the outlet (an inter-war replacement of the original) can still be seen at the corner of Redcliffe Hill and Colston Parade. This spout is now dry because of bomb damage in the lower sections of the pipe, but the upstream part still flows as far as Victoria Park in Windmill Hill. The stream now emerges here and flows into a beautiful water maze, built in 1984 to a design based on a roof boss in St. Mary Redcliffe.

The clerics who built Redcliffe Pipe shared the water with their parishioners – as was the case with most of the medieval conduits. Most people would have used it for drinking and cooking, but those with enough money and manpower to collect and heat sufficient water enjoyed baths. Many well-to-do folk possessed a wooden bathtub – rather like a huge barrel, often padded inside with linen. In this, the whole family and their guests bathed naked together. Many medieval pictures show them happily soaking, with a meal laid on a tray across the bath and musicians to entertain the party. It is hardly surprising that the words "stew" and "bordello" (which originally just meant "bath") gained unsavoury connotations.

Whatever they did with the water, Redcliffe people have always had a special affection for their ancient conduit, and to this day they trace its whole length on an annual Pipe Walk - a very jolly event which entails "bumping" participants on the conduit's marker stones. In 1990, the 800th Anniversary Pipe Walk was the occasion of particular celebration: the pilgrims heard that the bomb damage had at last been traced, and that Redcliffe Pipe might soon flow right up to St. Mary's again.

The water maze in Victoria Park, Windmill Hill

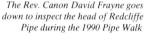

The Rev. Canon David Frayne goes down to inspect the head of Redcliffe Pipe during the 1990 Pipe Walk

"Bumping" the marker stones!

St. John's Conduit and Redcliffe Pipe are the best preserved of the medieval conduits, but there are substantial remains of many more. Gaunt's Hospital, St. Augustine's Abbey, St. Thomas' Church, the Hospital of St. John, Greyfriars, All Saints' Church, the Friary without Temple Gate, and Temple Church all had fresh water piped to them from the hills around Bristol. Most built their own conduits, but some were granted branch pipes (known as "feathers," because they were only supposed to be big enough to accommodate a goose quill) from neighbouring systems.

Quay Pipe – the longest and most spectacular of all the conduits – was not built by churchmen at all, but by the City. It piped water all the way from a spring near the Boiling Well at Ashley to the quayside near St. Stephen's Church. It was built in 1376 to service the booming city docks, and has a special place in the history of Bristol. It was from Quay Pipe, they say, that John Cabot filled up water casks to load on to his tiny ship, *The Matthew*, before setting sail for the New World.

Quay Pipe still brings spring water to the centre of the City, but as the outlet was dismantled in the 1930s, it now flows away into the Frome. The old pump head is kept at the offices of Bristol Waterworks.

Neptune's statue in 1787, on top of the
Temple Pipe outlet in Temple Street

Raven's Well, the source of Temple Pipe,
lies under the Three Lamps signpost

Like most of the conduits, the outlet of Quay Pipe was originally embellished with a stone water fountain or "castellette". None of the old castellettes is still in place, but all of them probably had decorated spouts and basins for dipping buckets into, like the restored outlets of St. John's Conduit and Redcliffe Pipe. Quay Pipe had a particularly "faire castellette" carved with a head of Momus, the god of laughter. This would have been particularly appropriate in the eighteenth century, when the Quay Pipe was made to run with wine on coronation days.

One of Bristol's most famous landmarks – the statue of Neptune which now stands at the head of St. Augustine's Reach – used to crown the castellette of Temple Pipe. This conduit was laid in 1366 to supply the Friary at Temple Gate and Temple Church, with a later extension to a public fountain in Temple Street. Neptune was erected over this last outlet in the 1720s. The fountain (and Neptune with it) was moved several times over the years. At the end of the last century, when Temple Pipe was severed by a new railway line and the outlet ran dry, Neptune was relocated again – and again – until he arrived at his present home in 1949.

The outlet of Temple Pipe can no longer be traced, but its source can still be found under the "Three Lamps" signpost at Totterdown. A narrow entrance leads down into

The discovery of the
Mikveh in Jacobs Wells

a maze of underground tunnels and reservoirs which collect the water from several springs. On the walls, the marks of the friars' pickaxes look as if they were made yesterday, and soot still coats the niches where they rested their candles.

Recently, some exciting discoveries in the Jacob's Wells area have revealed yet more of Bristol's ancient water system. When a house-holder in Gorse Lane accidentally uncovered a spring under the pavement by his door, investigation revealed that it flowed through a medieval stone-arched tunnel. This was the head of the Abbey Conduit, which flowed down Brandon Hill to St. Augustine's Abbey.

In 1986, Mr John Martelette made an even more startling discovery. Whilst demolish-ing a workshop at the junction of Jacob's Wells Road and Constitution Hill, he came across something which looked like an old fireplace, but was the entrance to a waterlogged, underground chamber. Fortunately, Bob Vaughan of the Temple Local History Group recognised its significance and oversaw an excavation. When the debris was cleared (including hundreds of batteries from the police bicycles which used to be stored thereabouts!), a spring of tepid water was found to gush into the chamber from a fis-sure in the rock. Steps lead down into the pool, and on the lintel above is carved the Hebrew

The new Jacob's Wells bottling plant

word "Sochalim" ("Flowing"). This is the oldest-known Hebrew inscription in Europe, dating from the eleventh or early twelfth century. Mr Martelette had uncovered the medieval Jewish ritual bath, or Mikveh, which probably gave Jacob's Well its name.

In the Middle Ages, Jews were largely restricted to dealing in finance (a matter so sordid that Christians were forbidden to soil their hands with it), so the Mikveh, which indicates a well-established Jewish community as far back as the eleventh century, is yet more evidence of Bristol's early importance as a commercial centre. Jews were expelled from England in 1290, so the Mikveh has probably lain neglected for 700 years, although the spring water continued to be used, and at one time supplied the public bath houses on Jacob's Wells Road. Now we can all sample it again, as it is to be bottled and sold commercially.

All the time, local archaeologists and historians are unearthing yet more underground evidence of medieval Bristol. In the light of each new discovery, it is becoming increasingly obvious that, far from being the "Dark Ages", this was one of the most vigorous and exciting periods in the City's history.

ACKNOWLEDGEMENTS

Many individuals and organisations have helped in the preparation of this book. We would particularly like to thank Julian Lea-Jones and the Temple Local History Group, who have given us access to all their original research. Special thanks also to Derek Fisher of Bygone Bristol, who allowed us to use rare photographs from his books *Bristol on Old Postcards*.

We would also like to thank the following for their invaluable help:

Robin Baxendale
Terry Bisgrove
Black Lion Costumiers
Dr A. Boycott
Ann Bradley
Bristol City Council Parks Department
Bristol Industrial Museum
Bristol United Press Ltd
British Cave Research Association
Mr G. Brook
Alan Bryant
Dave Cheeseley
City of Bristol Engineers Main Drainage Department
City of Bristol Museum and Art Gallery
City of Bristol Records Office
City of Bristol Reference Library
Don Cooper
John Cornwell
Peter G. Davey
Neil Dymond
Paul Elkins
Ann Hammond
Harveys of Bristol

Howells of Bristol
Noel Hooper
Andy King
Richard Lendrem
Don Loader
David Mander
Trevor Mason, British Aerospace
George Panayiotou and Andy Bennett, Tele Tape Video
Dave Price
Helen Reid
Rodway School Speleological Society
Bob Rutherford
Paul Singer
Bernard Smisson
David Street
Mrs S. Stoddard
Ken Thomas
Dr D.M.M. Thompson
Bruce Tyldesley
Warden and staff of Goldney House
Laurie Wason
Bob White